The Value of Animals

The Value of Animals

A CHRISTIAN PERSPECTIVE

J.M. Moore

This book is available for purchase on both electronic and paper media. Environmental impact considerations include the availability of the e-version, the use of the waste-reducing, on-demand printing method, and the potential environmental impact of the book's contents.

I have chosen not to communicate via social media.
"...a time to keep silence, and a time to speak" (Eccl 3:7)

TABLE OF CONTENTS

PREFACE: Balaam's Donkey

The inspiration to write *The Value of Animals* came to me as I was reading the story of Balaam and his donkey, which appears in the Book of Numbers (Num 22). Balaam was a diviner, a senseless peddler of GOD's wisdom, whom the king of Moab solicited to curse the then-advancing Israelites, because he and his people feared them. The king sent some messengers to Balaam, and for the diviner's fee they paid, Balaam asked GOD whether he should grant the king's request. GOD told Balaam to refuse, as the Israelites were His chosen people. The messengers delivered that message to the king, whereupon he sent a more distinguished delegation to Balaam, to make the same request but with a richer offer on their lips. Foolishly, Balaam sought GOD 's guidance again, as if He somehow might be swayed by the better pay. To dupe Balaam into having his foolishness revealed to him, GOD told him to go with the men, to their king, but to follow His commands along the way.

On the road to Moab, an angel of GOD appeared three times before Balaam and the donkey he was riding, to make them turn back. Each time, the donkey saw the angel but Balaam could not, making it impossible for him to know GOD's will. Each time, out of fear of the angel, the donkey altered its course or was otherwise uncooperative, and each time, Balaam struck the donkey for its apparent misbehavior. After the third incident, GOD enabled the donkey to speak. The donkey asked Balaam a couple of rhetorical questions to point out to him that he had been riding it all his life and that it was not in the habit of disobeying him. To conclude the episode, GOD revealed His angel to Balaam, who told Balaam that he would have killed him if his donkey had not avoided him. In this way, GOD made Balaam seem less perceptive than a donkey.

Balaam left a pathetic legacy. He instigated an episode of immorality among the Israelites (Num 31:16), and the Israelites executed him, under Moses (Num 31:8). The prophet Joshua mentions his execution and his sinful divining (Josh 13:22). In the New Testament, both Peter (2Pet 2:15) and Jude (Jude 11) liken certain depraved people to Balaam. Finally, in the Book of Revelation, Christ himself condemns Balaam's followers (Rev 2:14). In short, whatever Balaam's way, it led astray.

Another Aspect. As I reflected on Balaam's story, its main point, that GOD is steadfast in His commitments, was not lost on me; but I took note of another aspect of the story as well: the story presupposes that we have a sense that it is immoral to strike an animal for no good reason. GOD expects us to understand the indignation the donkey expresses when it begins to speak; He expects the story to make sense to us as it is written, without a direct statement that Balaam had sinned.

As a result, I felt called to study GOD's will as it relates to our treatment of animals. Like many people, I had read and heard certain, isolated biblical verses about our relationship with animals, but, on this occasion, I began to wonder whether those verses represented the sum total of GOD's guidance to us. The story of Balaam and his donkey suggests that one of our spiritual responsibilities is to treat animals kindly. I set out on a quest to confirm this suggestion, and it led me deep into the Bible and to many of its wonders and mysteries, e.g., prophecies of the Messiah; the visions of Daniel, Ezekiel, and John; the Christian spiritual hierarchy; the indispensable nature of faith; salvation through Christ; and the guiding presence of the Holy Spirit. GOD incorporates animals into countless verses of the Bible, and the high profile He has given them assures that they contribute much to His teachings.

Foundations. During the six days of Creation, GOD concerned Himself with the fundamentals of the universe. That our relationship with animals numbers among those fundamentals implies that we ought to give it considerable weight. GOD has seen to it that the sun will rise in the morning, that the moon and the stars will appear at night, and that there is habitable land on Earth. Now, it is our turn to pursue works such as conducting our foundational relationship with animals according to His will. Like the Book of Numbers' story of Balaam's donkey, other Scripture gives expression to the moral that GOD wants us to treat animals with care and grace and to appreciate the contributions they make to our world. Furthermore, Scripture reveals that, by His grace, the farther we move in that direction, the more blessed our experience of His infinite goodness will be.

My Prayers. I pray that *The Value of Animals* will benefit people and animals alike, a prayer that, the Bible teaches, harmonizes with GOD's plan for us. I feel blessed to have been chosen to undertake this project. It has given me a greater appreciation for the fathomless depth of GOD's Word. As I wrote the book, whenever I began to think that I had exhausted the reserve of wisdom Scripture had to offer on a topic, I would be disabused of the thought, as more wisdom would present itself. The Bible's store of wisdom is boundless, and writing *The Value of Animals* has strengthened my belief in its power. I pray that reading *The Value of Animals* will enrich your faith journey, as writing it has mine.

I have written the book with an eye toward making it accessible both to Christians and to non-Christians. In this way, I hope to have produced a work that will bear as much fruit as possible. I pray

i

that the book will prompt those of you who aren't Christians to take a first or a fresh look at the Christian faith. In his parable of the lost sheep, Jesus relates that your repentance would spark an especially joyous celebration in heaven (Lk 15:7). As any Christian will tell you, if my book were to play a part in that, then my efforts will have been worthwhile.

JMM
August 2023

PART I

GOD'S ANIMALS

1 GOD'S ANIMALS

Through their variety, their beauty, and their dynamic ways, animals glorify GOD, in all His power, His creativity, and His wisdom. The Bible imparts to us an appreciation not only for animals' outward lives but also for their inner lives, which GOD has enriched with perceptions, feelings, and desires. In the beginning, GOD established a special relationship between Himself and the animals, and He has maintained that relationship ever since. He always has played important roles in animals' lives, including the roles of keeper, protector, provider, and narrator, which is an offshoot of His role as author of the Bible, with all of its references to animals. GOD achieved a wonder when He created the animals. He gives His animal creation special attention, and His Book turns our attention to it, as well.

In the following passage, Psalm 104 celebrates GOD's work as Creator of the animals:

You have made the moon to mark the seasons;
the sun knows its time for setting.
You make darkness, and it is night,
when all the animals of the forest come creeping out.
The young lions roar for their prey, seeking their food from GOD.
When the sun rises, they withdraw,
and lie down in their dens.
People go out to their work
and to their labor until the evening.

O LORD, how manifold are your works!
In wisdom you have made them all;
the earth is full of your creatures. (Ps 104:19-24)

With verses like these, the Bible teaches us of the great wisdom and artistry GOD used in creating the animals. The Psalm would have benefitted Job...

In the Book of Job, the then-undeterred Job's doomed attempt to make a case against GOD left no room for the sort of reverence of Him that later would be expressed in Psalm 104, above. In His first response to Job, GOD takes him to task for his irreverence:

"Is it by your wisdom that the hawk soars and spreads its wings toward the south?
Is it at your command that the eagle mounts up and makes its nest on high?
It lives on the rock and makes its home in the fastness of the rocky crag.
From there it spies the prey; its eyes see it from far away.
Its young ones suck up blood; and where the slain are, there it is." (Job 39:26-30)

With this rebuttal, GOD cautions Job and us against overlooking the miraculous nature of the animal realm. He presents that realm as His own handiwork, or a work that pleases Him (Gen 1:20-25).

GOD's Handiwork. The Bible gives us entree into animals' minds, which feature awareness and a spectrum of emotions and drives. In the Book of Genesis, GOD tells of animals' fear and dread of us (Gen 9:1-2). In Psalm 42, He makes mention of a deer's longing for stream water (Ps 42:1). In Psalm 104, He relates that animals are dismayed when He veils His presence from them (Ps 104:29). Some Bible passages allow us to infer animals' mental states, as does this passage from the Book of Joel:

How the animals groan!
The herds of cattle wander about
because there is no pasture for them;
even the flocks of sheep are dazed.
To you, O LORD, I cry.
For fire has devoured
the pastures of the wilderness,
and flames have burned
all the trees of the field.
Even the wild animals cry to you,
because the watercourses have dried up,
and fire has devoured

the pastures of the wilderness. (Joel 1:18-20)

Joel could simply have written, "The animals are very hungry and very thirsty," but GOD inspired him to be more eloquent than that. These verses make it clear that the animals were indeed suffering from great hunger and great thirst, and the strength of Joel's inspired language makes their suffering tangible to us.

Within its pages, the Bible contains enraged bears (2Sam 17:8), panicked horses (Zech 12:4), frisky heifers (Jer 50:11), appalled sheep (Jer 49:20), and joyful wild asses (Isa 32:14). GOD crafted the animal realm in multiple dimensions, and He cares about it deeply.

GOD's Chosen Roles. In the Book of Genesis, GOD commands Noah to take with him on the ark at least one pair of every kind of animal (Gen 7:2-3). After the floodwaters recede, GOD makes a covenant not only with Noah, but also with the animals:

"As for me, I am establishing my covenant with you and your descendants after you, and with every living creature that is with you, the birds, the domestic animals, and every animal of the earth with you, as many as came out of the ark. I establish my covenant with you, that never again shall all flesh be cut off by the waters of a flood, and never again shall there be a flood to destroy the earth." (Gen 9:9-11)

GOD could have made this covenant with Noah alone. His inclusion of the animals indicates again that He holds them in special regard.

He acted as their keeper when He commanded Noah to take the animals aboard the ark. In this role, GOD watches over the entirety of His animal creation or over large groups of animals. Psalm 50 sums up the arrangement:

For every wild animal of the forest is mine,
the cattle on a thousand hills.
I know all the birds of the air,
and all that moves in the field is mine. (Ps 50:10-11)

These verses relate to GOD's role as keeper of all animals. In the Book of Matthew, Jesus echoes them when he says that not even a sparrow falls to earth apart from GOD (Mt 10:29). Meanwhile, the Book of Leviticus contains an example of GOD's playing the role of keeper of a subgroup of animals. Here, GOD describes the blessings He determined to bestow on the Israelites if they would keep His commandments:

"And I will grant peace in the land, and you shall lie down, and no one shall make you afraid; I will remove dangerous animals from the land, and no sword shall go through your land." (Lev 26:6)

The fulfillment of this promise would have involved the movement of a considerable number of animals, if not quite the number that would have taken part in a mass migration to the ark.

Just as GOD keeps His animals, He protects them. His role as protector comes through in Psalm 36:

Your steadfast love, O LORD, extends to the heavens,
your faithfulness to the clouds.
Your righteousness is like the mighty mountains,
your judgments are like the great deep;
you save humans and animals alike, O LORD. (Ps 36:5-6)

These verses stand in contrast to the verses that precede them, which describe the evil words and ways of the wicked; the Psalm includes the animals among those that GOD protects from such evildoers.

In the Book of Jonah, Jonah makes a couple of complaints, saying both times that on account of his anguish, it would be better for him to die than to go on living. In the first instance, he expresses anger over GOD's decision to spare the repentant city of Nineveh even though Jonah had proclaimed to the city that it soon would be overthrown (Jonah 4:1-3). Prior to the second instance, Jonah had left the city and encamped at a place where he could observe it and its fate. There, GOD produced a bush that shaded Jonah; but the next morning, GOD destroyed the bush. This prompted Jonah's second complaint and his second claim that he would rather die than continue to live. Here is GOD's reply to Jonah:

But GOD said to Jonah, "Is it right for you to be angry about the bush?" And he said, "Yes, angry enough to die."

Then the LORD said, "You are concerned about the bush, for which you did not labor and which you did not grow; it came into being in a night and perished in a night. And should I not be concerned about Nineveh, that great city, in which there are more than a hundred and twenty thousand persons who do not know their right hand from their left, and also many animals?" (Jonah 4:9-11)

With its closing words "and also many animals," this reply illustrates again that GOD acts as the animals' protector.

In Psalm 145, the psalmist writes that GOD's compassion extends to all of His Creation (Ps 145:9). That compassion shows when GOD plays the role of keeper of the animals, protector of the animals, or a third role, the role of provider to the animals. In the Psalm, GOD is portrayed as the provider of food:

The eyes of all look to you,
and you give them their food in due season.
You open your hand, satisfying the desire of every living thing. (Ps 145:15-16)

In Psalm 104, GOD is portrayed as the provider of water and shelter:

You make springs gush forth in the valleys;
they flow between the hills,
giving drink to every wild animal;
the wild asses quench their thirst.
By the streams, the birds of the air have their habitation;
they sing among the branches.
From your lofty abode you water the mountains;
the earth is satisfied with the fruit of your work. (Ps 104:10-13)

GOD provides for the animals, and throughout the Bible He also calls on them for help. He takes on the role of leader and gives animals the honor of helping Him to carry out His will here on earth. GOD led a ram to give its life so that Isaac would be spared Abraham's knife (Gen 22:13). He led Balaam's donkey to help Him teach Balaam a lesson (Num 22:28-34). He led a fish to swallow Jonah – and then to spew him out (Jonah 2:10). At various times, He led locusts, flies, frogs, and caterpillars to plague enemies of the Israelites, not least Egypt (Ex 8-10).

Another instance of GOD's leading animals takes shape during the Israelites' journey to the Promised Land. The people complained to GOD and to Moses that they had led them into the wilderness to die. They complained that there was no food other than GOD's manna from heaven, and they said that they detested the manna. In response, GOD led poisonous serpents to attack the people, who repented but still had to contend with the serpents. The people beseeched Moses to pray to GOD on their behalf, and he consented. GOD told Moses to sculpt a serpent and to put it on a pole; and He promised that anyone who looked at the serpent after being bitten would be cured (Num 21:5-9). Moses crafted the serpent, and the bitten were healed; and, famously, this episode is memorialized in modern-day, medical-related signs and logos that feature images of the snake.

Finally, as the animals' "narrator," GOD involves Himself in animals' daily lives just as He does in His other roles. GOD's Word is forever enlightening us, guiding us, challenging us, inspiring us, awing us, and saving us. The animals of the Bible contribute to its power, and we may appreciate them anew every time the Bible mentions them. So, by way of His Book, GOD invites us to remain mindful of the animals, and by His design at Creation, our mindfulness can have profound effects on their lives. Through the mindful, then, GOD augments His ongoing participation in animals' lives, and this is one of the ways in which His Word is a Living Word.

2 THE LIVING WORD

The Bible teems with animals. The verses mentioned in *The Value of Animals* are but a few of the many that speak of them. GOD incorporates animals into the Bible by telling us about historical events that involve them and by drawing comparisons between animals and others – others in heaven, in hell, and here on earth. With a few exceptions, biblical animals are accepted as they are; on the whole, GOD shows us that there is a place for the animals in His Design, even the lowliest of them and even when they behave in befuddling ways.

Chapter 1 made mention of historical events that GOD recounts in order to teach us with them. GOD taught Jonah and us a lesson in being humble before Him, a lesson in taking the importance of others – including animals – into account when we assess our own importance (Jonah 4:9-11). Earlier on, having instructed Noah to build his ark so big that it would fit at least two animals of each and every kind (Gen 6:19), GOD impressed upon us how profound Noah's faith was. Noah's faith sustained him as he undertook his daunting and what must have seemed quixotic task, and ever since, we have regarded him as a paragon of faith. Once more, the stories of Noah and Jonah, as well as the story of Balaam (Num 22), illustrate GOD's method of teaching us via history and its animals.

Comparisons. The animal world proved a rich resource for comparisons that enliven and strengthen the Bible. Variously, the Bible compares Satan to a prowling lion (1Pet 5:8) and the unsaved to dogs (Rev 22:15); and it compares GOD Himself to a roaring lion (Hos 11:10) and to a soaring eagle (Ex 19:4). When it comes to comparing humans to animals, GOD does so, for instance, by making direct comparisons or by using object lessons.

In Psalm 22, GOD inspired David to make a direct comparison between himself and an animal:

But I am a worm, and not human;
scorned by others, and despised by the people.
All who see me mock at me;
they make mouths at me, they shake their heads;
"Commit your cause to the LORD; let Him deliver you –
let Him rescue the one in whom He delights!" (Ps 22:6-8)

Being a persecuted believer made David feel like a worm, one of the most repulsive of animals. Meanwhile, in the Book of Proverbs, GOD makes His point with one of the most repulsive of animal behaviors:

Like a dog that returns to its vomit
is a fool who reverts to his folly. (Prov 26:11)

As unpleasant as this behavior is, the comparison and, therefore, the lesson it teaches leave an indelible impression on us. If we ever confront a situation to which this Proverb applies, its unsavory imagery virtually assures that we will recall it.

Other direct comparisons make use of more palatable animal traits. For example, the prophet Isaiah draws on the GOD-given magnificence of the eagle to express a message of faith:

Even youths will faint and be weary,
and the young will fall exhausted;
but those who wait for the LORD shall
renew their strength,
they shall mount up with wings like eagles,
they shall run and not be weary,
they shall walk and not faint. (Isa 40:30-31)

In the Book of Exodus, GOD is compared to a soaring eagle; here, the faithful are compared to an eagle taking flight, strengthened by their faith.

Object Lessons. The Book of Proverbs contains the following object lesson, which makes some observations about the ant world and then applies them to our world:

Go to the ant, you lazybones,
consider its ways and be wise.
Without having any chief

4

or official or ruler,
it prepares its food in summer,
and gathers its sustenance in harvest.
How long will you lie there, O Lazybones?
When will you rise from your sleep?
A little sleep, a little slumber,
a little folding of the hands to rest,
and poverty will come upon you like a robber,
and want, like an armed warrior. (Prov 6:6-11)

The ant's smallness and simplicity give this lesson size and sophistication. The Proverb challenges us to ask ourselves, "If the tiny ants can be organized and industrious, why can't we, with our superior brawn and brains?" The Proverb also answers the question: if we have failed to be organized and industrious, it is not unlikely that we have succumbed to laziness. In this way, GOD's Design allows the behavior of an insect to impart wisdom to us.

Chapter 1 describes GOD's efforts to open Job's eyes to the miraculous nature of His Creation. Following on those efforts, GOD brings the ostrich into focus:

"The ostrich's wings flap wildly,
though its pinions lack plumage.
For it leaves its eggs to the earth,
and lets them be warmed on the ground,
forgetting that a foot may crush them,
and that a wild animal may trample them.
It deals cruelly with its young, as if they were not its own,
though its labor should be in vain;
yet it has no fear,
because GOD has made it forget wisdom
and given it no share in understanding.
When it spreads its plumes aloft,
it laughs at the horse and its rider." (Job 39:13-18)

Here, GOD invites Job and us to contemplate the mystery of His miraculous Creation. The ostrich flaps its wings but does not fly. Rather, it runs, faster than "the horse and its rider;" it lacks the wisdom to fear them; and its open-beaked hissing makes it look and sound as if it laughs at them. The ostrich deals cruelly with its young. Ostriches typically live in small groups consisting of a male; a dominant female; sometimes a small number of subordinate females; and their chicks. On occasion, the adults of one of these family groups will face off against the adults of another, and the winning group will gain possession of the other group's chicks. The losing group will relinquish its chicks "as if they were not its own," and they will depart, unfazed by the chicks' absence.

With this object lesson, GOD subtly helps us to understand how small a part in understanding we ourselves have been given. Only GOD could conceive of an animal such as the ostrich. Only GOD could envision a world in which such an animal has a place. Job repeatedly took the wonders of Creation, including the unlikely ostrich, for granted and tried to box the Creator into his worldview. Ultimately, though, he saw the errors in his way of thinking, and he humbled himself before the LORD:

Then Job answered the LORD:
"I know that you can do all things,
and that no purpose of yours can be thwarted.
'Who is this that hides counsel without knowledge?'
Therefore, I have uttered what I did not understand,
things too wonderful for me, which I did not know." (Job 42:1-3)

Here, the Bible adds to the improbability of the ostrich. In addition to fitting it into His Design in the first place, GOD foresaw that this irrational animal could help a troubled man like Job to find his peace with Him.

Further, even to this day, by giving the ostrich its place in His Living Word, GOD continues to challenge us in novel ways with it. With little doubt, the ostrich of the Bible is the Arabian ostrich, which lived in biblical lands. The Arabian ostrich went extinct in 1941. Long before, upon the Flood's having subsided, GOD gave Noah the following instructions:

"Go out of the ark, you and your wife, and your sons and your sons' wives with you. Bring out with you every living thing that is with you of all flesh – birds and animals and every creeping thing that creeps on the earth – so that they may abound on the earth, and be fruitful and multiply on the earth." (Gen 8:16-17)

With the extinction of the Arabian ostrich, GOD's wish that every kind of animal abound suffered a setback. The extinction calls us to give even greater weight to questions such as whether we can take additional steps to save other animals from the same fate.

Acceptance. The Bible accepts the animals, GOD's creations, for what they are. It does not condemn the dog for returning to its vomit, as revolting as that behavior is to us. It only presents the behavior as one that has a place in GOD's Creation, a Creation that the Book of Job teaches us we do not fully understand. The Bible does not blame the worm for being almost untouchable, nor, on the other hand, does it give the eagle credit for being so strong and majestic-looking; in the Bible, as in life, the eagle's strength and majesty glorify GOD, and not the eagle itself. The Bible sees no contradiction in the lion's roar conjuring GOD's might, and its prowling, Satan's evil. GOD designed animals – even the misunderstood ostrich – to be what they are. We might roll our eyes at them, we might marvel at them, we might laugh at them, we might cry for them; but we seldom condemn them or laud them for behaving as they do. Our non-judgmental acceptance of them mirrors the Bible's treatment of them. They constitute an important part of GOD's Creation, and in verses throughout the Bible, GOD tells us that His Creation is good.

Exceptions. Now, in matters of acceptable behavior, the Bible does contain a handful of exceptions first to the rule that GOD does not hold His animals to standards of human morality, and, second, to the converse rule that He does not encourage humans to model their behavior on animal behavior – at least not of the unredeeming sort. As to the first of these two categories, chapter 7 of *The Value of Animals* explores the possibility that it has implications for the spiritual realm.

An exception in that first category appears in the Book of Exodus. In preparation for His appearance to Moses on Mount Sinai, GOD gives Moses these instructions:

"You shall set limits for the people all around, saying, 'Be careful not to go up the mountain or to touch the edge of it. Any who touch the mountain shall be put to death. No hand shall touch them, but they shall be stoned or shot with arrows; whether animal or human being, they shall not live.' When the trumpet sounds a long blast, they may go up on the mountain." (Ex 19:12-13)

The first sentences of this passage read as if GOD was setting limits for the people alone; He did not hint that the limits would apply to animals as well. The surprising inclusion of animals signals to us what an extraordinary event GOD's appearance to Moses would be. Even a hapless animal would have to pay the price for encroaching on GOD's holiness, and by virtue of that, the animals contribute to the Living Word's tale of one of the most important events that ever will occur in the history of the world.

Whereas GOD's Mount Sinai prohibition holds animals to a human standard of behavior, a second exception rewards men for behaving like animals. In the Book of Judges, as Gideon and his troops stood in position to attack the Midianites, GOD commanded Gideon to thin his ranks, to ensure that the Israelites would give Him credit for the promised victory, and not an Israeli army with superior numbers. At GOD's command, Gideon faithfully took his troops to the spring of Harod, where GOD gave him these instructions:

...the LORD said to Gideon, "All those who lap the water with their tongues, as a dog laps, you shall put to one side; all those who kneel down to drink, putting their hands to their mouths, you shall put on the other side." (Judg 7:5)

Three hundred soldiers lapped as a dog laps, and those three hundred were selected to carry out the attack. Perhaps by lapping the water, the soldiers indicated, unknowingly, that in battle they would fight like dogs. Although Midian's troops greatly outnumbered Israel's, Israel conquered Midian, and GOD received the credit. So, by behaving like animals, the troops were given the honor of participating in a victory for the LORD (Judg 7:19-25) [though, in the final analysis, all they had to do was to blow some trumpets and to shout a few times, as the Israelites did to capture Jericho (Josh 6:20)].

While they tell of exceptions to the normal rules of conduct, the stories of the Mount Sinai animals and of the spring-of-Harod soldiers have an important element in common with the other biblical passages that mention animals: in all of them, GOD uses animals to make His wisdom and His guidance more accessible to us. Exceptionally memorable, the exceptions cast light and not doubt.

Solomon's Wisdom. To conclude, in the following passage from the First Book of Kings, the Bible gives us a glimpse of one of its own contributors in action:

GOD gave Solomon very great wisdom, discernment, and breadth of understanding as vast as the sand on the seashore, so that Solomon's wisdom surpassed the wisdom of all the people of the east, and all the wisdom of Egypt. He was wiser than anyone else, wiser than Ethan the Ezrahite, and Heman, Calcol, and Darda, children of Mahol; his fame spread throughout all the surrounding nations. He composed three thousand proverbs, and his songs numbered a thousand and five. He would speak of trees, from the cedar that is in Lebanon to the hyssop that grows in the wall; he would speak of animals and birds and reptiles and fish. People came from all the nations to hear the wisdom of Solomon; they came from all the kings of the earth who had heard of his wisdom. (1 Kings 4:29-34)

Solomon's GOD-given wisdom turns toward the animal world an appreciative eye that sees beyond acceptance alone. Through other verses, the Bible reveals how a lack of intelligence can seal the case for intelligent design; it advises against making the same mistake twice; it asserts the inviolability of GOD's holiness; and it prescribes a faith-based method for selecting the best soldiers from an army. In composing these lessons, GOD has made them unforgettable to us by highlighting aspects of His animal creation. In His role as narrator and in all the other roles He plays in their lives, GOD has a close and active relationship with His animals. When He populated the Bible with them, He enlisted them to make an ongoing and eternal contribution to the perfection of His Perfect Book.

3 DOMINION

The Bible makes it clear that the character of any instance of dominion depends on the holder of dominion. In the hands of GOD, dominion is exercised with benevolence; in the hands of the wicked, it is enforced with threats and intimidation. The Bible also makes it clear that GOD expects us to exercise our dominion over animals in His manner of exercising dominion.

Three Psalms. In the three Psalms, 19, 22, and 23 together, GOD inspired David to write about both dominion in the hands of GOD and dominion in the hands of the wicked. In Psalm 19, David asks GOD to keep him from misreading His law:

But who can detect their errors?
Clear me from hidden faults.
Keep back your servant also from the insolent;
do not let them have dominion over me.
Then I shall be blameless,
and innocent of great transgression. (Ps 19:12-13)

David recognizes the danger of coming under the influence of the insolent: it leads to transgression. Psalm 22, in which he calls himself a worm, includes a prayer for relief. David promises GOD that he will sing His praises when He delivers him from his enemies:

From you comes my praise in the great congregation;
My vows I will pay before those who fear Him.
The poor shall eat and be satisfied;
those who seek Him shall praise the LORD.
May your hearts live forever!

All the ends of the earth shall remember
and turn to the LORD;
and all the families of the nations
shall worship before Him.
For dominion belongs to the LORD,
and He rules over the nations. (Ps 22:25-28)

The very next Psalm, the beloved Psalm 23, begins, "The LORD is my shepherd; I shall not want" – one of the many biblical verses that portray GOD as a shepherd who exercises dominion righteously over His followers, or flock. So, on the scale of nations (Ps 22, above) down to the scale of individuals (Ps 23), the tone of dominion in GOD's hands is sweet; it calls for celebration. Whereas dominion in the hands of the insolent corrupts, dominion in the hands of GOD unites. Whereas the fruits of the former are transgression and blame, under GOD the poor eat and are satisfied.

A Prophecy. In a speech that marked his son Solomon's succession to the throne, it was GOD's absolute dominion that David chose to extol, praying that the new king would be an obedient subject, a humble administrator of that highest of dominions (1Chr 29:10-19). And GOD inspired Isaiah to prophesy as follows concerning the long-term fate of David's crown, which, for a moment in history, would become a crown of thorns (Mt 1:6-16; Jn 19:2):

For a child has been born for us,
a son given to us;
authority rests upon his shoulders;
and he is named
Wonderful Counselor, Mighty GOD,
Everlasting Father, Prince of Peace.
His authority shall grow continually,
and there shall be endless peace
for the throne of David and his kingdom.
He will establish it and uphold it
with justice and with righteousness
from this time onward and forevermore.
The zeal of the LORD of hosts will do this. (Isa 9:6-7)

In this passage, the honor to David and his posterity resides not in the power of their dominion but in its peace. Isaiah describes a godly dominion; his description naturally takes on a joyous tone. With his embrace of such dominion, the notorious warrior David (1Chr 22:6-10) surely found for himself the peace of knowing GOD, and he surely founded for himself a legacy of peace, as Isaiah foretold that it would be.

The Visions of Daniel and John. In the Book of Daniel, Daniel has a vision that, like the Psalms above, shows that the power of dominion can be harnessed for either good or evil. The first part of Daniel's vision features four terrifying beasts that were given dominion but then were stripped of it. In the latter part of his vision, Daniel sees the holder of dominion who was installed in their place:

As I watched in the night visions,
I saw one like a human being
coming with the clouds of heaven.
And he came to the Ancient One
and was presented before Him.
To him was given dominion
and glory and kingship,
that all peoples, nations, and languages
should serve him.
His dominion is an everlasting dominion
that shall not pass away,
and his kingship is one
that shall never be destroyed. (Dan 7:13-14)

Jesus referred to himself as "the Son of Man" (e.g., Mt 8:20, 12:8), or "one like a human being," and after he was arrested, he reiterated Daniel's prophecy to the High Priest Caiaphas (Mt 26:64). In the following verses, the Book of Revelation also indicates that Jesus is the king that Daniel envisioned, who will come with the clouds of heaven:

...To him who loves us and freed us from our sins by his blood, and made us to be a kingdom, priests serving his GOD and Father, to him be glory and dominion forever and ever. Amen.

Look! He is coming with the clouds;
every eye will see him,
even those who pierced him;
and on his account all the tribes of the earth will wail.

So it is to be. Amen. (Rev 1:5-7)

The dominion John prays for here could not differ more from the dominion that initially haunted Daniel's vision, the dominion of the four great beasts that came out of the sea. It is the dominion of the Son of Man for which John prays. The former dominion would have been exercised with cruelty, terror, oppression, and evil; the latter will be exercised with kindness, caring, consideration, and goodness. While our dominion over animals can't match the perfection of Christ's dominion over us, the Bible encourages us to make ours resemble Christ's and contrast with the dominion of the insolent or of nightmarish beasts. The Bible does this through direct guidance, through examples of the moral treatment of animals, and, in a cautionary way, through examples of the immoral.

Expectations of Moral Treatment. As mentioned in the preface, when the angel of GOD confronted that blind diviner Balaam, the angel expressed outrage over his mistreatment of his donkey:

The angel of the LORD said to him, "Why have you struck your donkey these three times? I have come out as an adversary, because your way is perverse before me. The donkey saw me and turned away from me these three times. If it had not turned away from me, surely just now I would have killed you and let it live." (Num 22:32-33)

These verses show that the angel expected Balaam to treat his donkey better, and the angel's expectation has backing in the Book of Proverbs:

The righteous know the needs of their animals,
but the mercy of the wicked is cruel. (Prov 12:10)

Balaam treated his donkey with cruel mercy. When the donkey asked him why he had struck it, Balaam not only failed to acknowledge his cruelty but also said that he would have killed the donkey if he had been carrying a sword. So, Balaam's show of mercy consisted of his striking his donkey, wishing it dead, and letting it live only because he lacked a sword. Balaam's mistreatment of his donkey compounded his wickedness, and the tale continues to educe in us disdain for his perverse ways.

The Bible gives further guidance that, like Proverbs 12:10 above, steers us away from the sin of Balaam and toward the godliness that escaped him. When GOD decrees that the Israelites rest on the seventh day, He explains that they should do so, in part, to relieve their oxen and their donkeys from their work for a day (Ex 23:12). Additionally, in the Fourth Commandment, GOD expressly prohibits the working of livestock on the Sabbath (Ex 20:10). In the Book of Isaiah, GOD promises happiness to those who let their oxen and their donkeys range freely (Isa 32:20). Thus, GOD numbers rest and relief among animals' needs, needs the righteous know and fulfill for their animals.

From another selection of direct lessons about the moral treatment of animals, the sanctity of the bond between mothers and their offspring emerges as a theme. When He spoke to Moses on Mount Sinai, GOD commanded that lambs, kids, and calves must be allowed to remain with their mothers for at least seven days before He would accept them as sacrifices (Lev 22:27). He also commanded that animals not be slaughtered on the same day as their young (Lev 22:28); and He commanded that a mother bird be let go if her eggs or her fledglings have been taken from her nest (Deut 22:6-7). GOD tells us to abide by the last of these so that "it may go well with you and you may live long." This echoes the reason GOD gives us in the Fifth Commandment to honor our parents, so that "your days may be long in the land that the LORD your GOD is giving you" (Ex 20:12). This similarity adds emphasis to the Bible's message that the special bond between mothers and their young – even between mother animals and their young – is a gift from GOD, a gift that we should handle with care.

Examples of Moral Treatment. Biblical accounts of interactions between humans and animals show that the faithful care about animals and play roles in their lives similar to the roles GOD plays in them, including the roles of leader, keeper, narrator, protector, and provider. In the Book of Judges, chapter 15, Samson takes on the role of leader. At the time, GOD desired to deal a blow to the Philistines, who held dominion over Israel, and at His behest (Judg 14:3-4), Samson married a Philistine woman. At the wedding feast Samson put a riddle to the Philistines in attendance, and he bet them sixty linen and festal garments that they could not solve the riddle within the seven days allotted for the feast. The Philistines struggled to solve it, and eventually they approached Samson's bride for the solution. She gave it to them, making Samson angry. Samson left for his father's house.

When Samson eventually returned, he learned that his wife's father had given her to another man. This angered Samson again and spurred him to action. The action he took cast him in the role of leader of three hundred foxes. Samson caught the foxes and paired them up. He turned each pair tail to tail and fixed a torch to each pair of tails. Then Samson lit the torches and released the foxes into the Philistines' grain fields, vineyards, and olive groves, burning them all down. This incident would propel Samson to a pair of miraculous, superhuman shows of force against the Philistines. So, just as, for example, GOD led the fish that swallowed Jonah in a holy mission (Jonah 1:17), Samson led the foxes in a holy mission, to strike back at Israel's oppressors.

When GOD drew all the animals to Noah, Noah took on the roles of provider, keeper, and leader. At GOD's command, Noah supplied his ark with enough food to provide for the animals (Gen 6:21). Noah played an especially important role as keeper, by ensuring that each kind of animal would be able to multiply on earth again. As the floodwaters receded, Noah played the role of leader to a dove:

Then he sent out the dove from him, to see if the waters had subsided from the face of the ground; but the dove found no place to set its foot, and it returned to him, to the ark, for the waters were still on the face of the whole earth. So he put out his hand and took it and brought it into the ark with him. He waited another seven days, and again he sent out the dove from the ark; and the dove came back to him in the evening, and there in its beak was a freshly plucked olive leaf; so Noah knew that the waters had subsided from the earth. Then he waited another seven days, and he sent out the dove; and it did not return to him anymore. (Gen 8:8-12)

In these epochal verses of simple beauty, Noah's undeniably gentle handling of the dove hints that he treated all of the animals on the ark kindly. In this way, together with the other holy people of the Bible, Noah sets a positive tone for the dominion over animals that GOD would reestablish for us soon thereafter.

GOD expects us to look to Him for a model of dominion. He has placed His trust in us to work with animals, as Samson did, rather than against them; to take their needs into account, as the righteous do;

and to handle them gently, as Noah did. In regard to the role of narrator, it is played by the faithful human writers of the Bible, whom GOD inspired to draw so effectively on the animal realm in their writing. In regard to the role of protector, it is played by herders and others, with great devotion and heartfelt care. Nonetheless, despite the prevalence of such models of humanity, sometimes it is challenging to reconcile certain elements of the Bible with its overarching imperative that we treat animals mercifully.

4 SUFFERING; SACRIFICE

In times of trouble, neither the humans of the Bible nor the animals escaped injury. Nevertheless, unless some higher purpose of GOD's was manifestly at risk, the inhumane treatment of animals was judged harshly. The Bible's disapproval of inhumane treatment extends to excesses in any context whatsoever, including war, individuals' confrontations with animals, and rites of sacrifice. The last of these factors greatly into the Bible's narrative. The practice of making offerings to GOD got off to an inauspicious start when it set the stage for Cain's murdering Abel, as related in the Book of Genesis. GOD later would lay out His sacrificial laws in detail, giving people the opportunity to make sacrifices in the spirit He intended. That spirit placed great value on sacrificial animals' lives; it even gave people incentives to sacrifice less. However, people proved incapable of honoring the spirit of GOD's law, and they fell into the habit of using sacrifice as a crutch. Despite a drumbeat in the Old Testament of clarifications, lamentations, exhortations, and condemnations, people could not manage to effect godly sacrifice with consistency. Nevertheless, GOD ultimately did not allow animals to be sacrificed in vain: the failure of the institution of animal sacrifice holds lessons that continue to edify us today.

Suffering. The Bible gives many accounts of animals' suffering or perishing beside their owners during unsettled times. For instance, it documents armies' engaging in at least two wartime practices cruel to animals: the placement of stumbling blocks and hamstringing. Stumbling blocks were positioned so as to trip up an enemy's charging war horses and to break their legs. To hamstring an animal means to cripple it by severing its hamstrings, and by hamstringing them, armies would disable enemies' war horses and draft animals. King David hamstrung the chariot horses of King Hadadezer of Zobah (1Chr 18:4), and Joshua also hamstrung enemy horses (Josh 11:9). Nonetheless, in keeping with its message of mercy, the Bible condemns the arbitrary infliction of suffering via hamstringing. For example, David spared one hundred of Hadadezer's horses. Relatedly, Jacob addressed the following deathbed message to two of his twelve sons:

Simeon and Levi are brothers;
weapons of violence are their swords.
May I never come into their council;
may I not be joined to their company —
for in their anger they killed men,
and at their whim they hamstrung oxen.
Cursed be their anger, for it is fierce,
and their wrath, for it is cruel!
I will divide them in Jacob,
and scatter them in Israel. (Gen 49:5-7)

With this negative assessment of his sons' abuses, Jacob added his own to the Bible's denunciations of such inhumanity.

Even when holy people of the Bible killed animals with GOD's blessing, they did so without behaving in hateful ways. In the Book of Judges, when Samson was attacked by a lion, he tore the lion apart "as one might tear apart a kid" (i.e., the offspring of a goat) (Judg 14:6). This startling comparison illustrates how strong Samson was; the entire episode illustrates that holy people do not torture animals. Samson did not prolong the lion's suffering; acting in self-defense, he quickly killed it.

On Mount Sinai, GOD told Moses that the Israelites were to sacrifice or to redeem to Him all firstborn livestock that were males (Ex 13:12-16). GOD commanded this as a way to remind the Israelites that He had led them out of slavery in Egypt and that, on the eve of their emancipation, He had killed Egypt's firstborn sons and livestock. GOD said that donkeys had to be redeemed via the redemption of a sheep, and He went on to say that if they were not redeemed, for lack of a sheep, their necks were to be broken. Breaking a donkey's neck would kill the donkey instantly. Thus, GOD again required the Israelites to use a humane method of killing, a method that would not cause the donkeys to suffer.

In a similar vein, among His instructions for properly performing the rites of sacrifice, GOD included these:

If your offering to the LORD is a burnt offering of birds, you shall choose your offering from turtledoves or pigeons. The priest shall bring it to the altar and wring off its head, and turn it into smoke on the altar; and its blood shall be drained out against the side of the altar. He shall remove its crop with its contents and throw it at the east side of the altar, in the place for ashes. He shall tear it open by its wings without severing it. Then the priest shall turn it into smoke on the altar, on the wood that is on the fire; it is a burnt offering, an offering by fire of pleasing odor to the LORD. (Lev 1:14-17)

At first, the prescribed method of killing the bird, by wringing off its head, might seem cruel, but in fact it would have caused the bird little suffering. Wringing off a bird's head would kill the bird instantly; and so, GOD mercifully required the priests to behave in a humane manner and to bring the birds quickly to an end. Mercy and humanity – the discussion that follows shows that these and other morals are the undercurrent throughout the Bible's chronicle of animal sacrifice and its demise.

Sin, Guilt and Well-being Offerings. In general terms, the types of sacrifices lay Israelites most often presented to GOD included sin, guilt, and well-being offerings. The meat of sacrificed animals was not wasted. Except in the case of whole burnt offerings, which were intended solely for GOD, the meat was eaten, and the sacrifices helped to sustain the priesthood, whose members GOD forbade to own land or to accumulate wealth (Num 18:8-24). Guilt and sin offerings purified GOD's sanctuary of offerors' guilt or sin; the sins and the guilt of the Israelites contaminated the very place where GOD resided among them – first the Tabernacle and later the Temple (e.g., Num 19:13; Lev 16:16). Only priests and their sons were allowed to eat the meat of sin and guilt offerings, a food so holy that it was designated a "food of GOD" (Lev 21:22).

When GOD commanded the Israelites to "reverence My Sanctuary" (Lev 26:2), He effectively warned them against, for example, engaging in a cycle of casual sin and perfunctory sacrifice. GOD wanted the Israelites not to sin, not to defile His Sanctuary, in the first place; and this desire is reflected in His laws relating to the manner in which sin and guilt offerings were to be made. Firstly, the laws permitted only unblemished animals to be made sin and guilt offerings (e.g., Lev 6:6). This requirement prevented offerors from using their guilt or sin as an occasion to cull their flocks or herds; the sacrificed animals would have had the greatest economic value to them.

Secondly, GOD surely intended the sacrificial rite to be a moving experience to the offeror. Offerors stood at the altar and laid a hand on the animal to be sacrificed (e.g., Lev 4:33), an act that should have made them feel humble, thoughtful, and grateful to the animal. To feel the wool or the fur of an animal that was about to die for them would have made the ritual personal – and intensely so if the animal was from their own herd or flock and, so, known well to them. Ideally, this would have given them a feeling of humility; and they would have recognized that only by GOD's grace were they permitted to rectify a morally untenable situation through the animal, whose warmth and breath and movement they could feel at their fingertips. It would have made them grateful to the animal for its role in scrubbing the stain of their transgressions from GOD's presence and they would have kept the animal in their thoughts after it had been sacrificed. Ideally – that is, if the offerors honored the spirit of GOD's sacrificial law – all of this would have inspired them to treat animals mercifully and to become better people in general, as they would have thought twice before they behaved in ways that would have made further guilt or sin offerings necessary.

In comparison to sin and guilt offerings, GOD placed slightly fewer restrictions on sacrifices of well-being, which comprised the freewill offering, the votive offering, and the thanksgiving offering (Lev 7:11-18). In some cases, He permitted animals with certain defects to be sacrificed (Lev 22:23), and He allowed ordinary Israelites to eat the meat of well-being sacrifices, "...rejoicing in the presence of the LORD your GOD in all your undertakings" (Deut 12:18). Well-being offerings were carried out in much the same way as sin and guilt offerings, and they predominated at the various festivals on the Israelites' calendar.

All in all, by addressing the particulars, GOD promoted the best outcome for both the sacrificed and the sacrificer. GOD's instructions pointed the way to rites of a personal and intimate nature, rites that demanded the considerate treatment of animals.

Right Sacrifices. In Psalm 51, David asks GOD to give him the blessings directly that He designed sacrifice to bring. He asks GOD to blot out his transgressions, to cleanse him of his sins, and to create in him a clean heart. Then, in the following verses, he demonstrates that he grasps the spirit of godly sacrifice:

O LORD, open my lips,
and my mouth will declare your praise.
For you have no delight in sacrifice;
if I were to give a burnt offering, you would not be pleased.
The sacrifice acceptable to GOD is a broken spirit;
a broken and contrite heart, O GOD, you will not despise.

Do good to Zion in your good pleasure;
rebuild the walls of Jerusalem,
then you will delight in right sacrifices,

in burnt offerings and whole burnt offerings;
then bulls will be offered on your altar. (Ps 51:15-19)

The sacrifices David promises would have been sacrifices of well-being. Right sacrifices were made with a "contrite heart." If GOD would rebuild the walls of Jerusalem, which had been destroyed in war, the Israelites would be humble before Him when they made their sacrifices. Having been delivered from the torment of displacement, they would not use sacrifice merely to create the appearance of honoring GOD with it; they would honor GOD in their hearts first, and then make sacrifices from the heart. Acts of cruelty toward the sacrificial animals would undermine the people's efforts to cultivate in themselves humility, integrity, and contrition. Recall the angel's rebuking the spiritually oblivious Balaam for having struck his donkey as he did (Num 22:32). The Bible consistently decries the cruel treatment of animals; right sacrifices surely were conducted with mercy.

In the books of the Bible, David's vision of right sacrifices is realized at some of the high points along the uneven trajectory of the Temple's history. The Temple was the soul of Jerusalem; the Holy City's holiness derived from GOD's presence in the Temple. The construction or restoration of the Temple breathed new life into the city, infusing with Spirit what had been mere stonework. In recognition of David's confiding to Solomon the task of building the Temple, more than three thousand animals were sacrificed (1Chr 29:21-22). At the dedication of Solomon's Temple, so many sacrifices were made that they could not be counted (2Chr 5:6), and Solomon offered one hundred forty-two thousand additional sacrifices when GOD first entered the Temple (2Chr 7:5). On the occasion of King Hezekiah's restoration of the Temple, so many offerings were made that the priests could not keep up with the demand to skin them (2Chr 29:34). During the special Passover and Festival of Unleavened Bread that followed, nineteen thousand animals were sacrificed (2Chr 30:23-27). Under King Josiah, to celebrate the return of the Ark of the Covenant to the Temple, forty-one thousand four hundred sacrifices were made (2Chr 35:7-9).

Exclusively or with very few exceptions, such great numbers were reserved for ceremonies related to the Temple. On their own, humans could not have carried out all of these sacrifices at the altar in the time frames the Bible indicates; and this suggests that GOD Himself must have played a role in seeing them through. Perhaps GOD was so moved by the people's shows of generosity and faith that He resolved to assure that all who bore offerings would be acknowledged; for He produced miracles at these Temple openings, surely enabling the sort of right, merciful sacrifices that David envisioned with such confidence, above, in Psalm 51.

Unholy Sacrifice. Ultimately and of necessity, the Bible drowns out even genuine expressions of faith, like those celebrating the Temple, with the hammering of its commentaries on the widespread corruption of GOD's sacrificial laws. To begin with, before GOD articulated those laws, Cain fatefully killed Abel because GOD accepted an offering Abel made but rejected the offering Cain made at the same time (Gen 4:2-5). Having become a shepherd, Abel offered the fat of a lamb; having become a "tiller of the ground," Cain offered some of his produce. GOD later would codify offerings like Cain's in His law, as, for example, in the second chapter of the Book of Leviticus, which covers grain offerings.

As to Abel's offering, in time, it would be written in the Book of Hebrews that Abel's faith made it acceptable to GOD (Heb 11:4). Meanwhile, GOD disregarded Cain's offering because He detected the evil in Cain. Noting Cain's irreverent reaction to His disregard for the offering, GOD said to him, *"Why are you angry, and why has your countenance fallen? If you do well, will you not be accepted? And if you do not do well, sin is lurking at the door; its desire is for you, but you must master it." (Gen 4:6-7)*. In spite of this wisdom, Cain proceeded to murder Abel.

One of the Proverbs reads, "The sacrifice of the wicked is an abomination; / how much more when brought with evil intent" (Prov 21:27). This Proverb, the wording of which connotes animal sacrifice, can be applied to Cain's offering, of produce, with almost no stretching. Cain made his offering in the spirit of one who would murder the innocent. His offering was an abomination.

Like the story of Cain and Abel, the story of Saul, in the First Book of Samuel, gives us an early sign that people were destined to follow the letter of sacrificial law, but not the spirit of it. Saul defied the LORD twice for the sake of sacrificial ritual. The first time, Saul had led an Israelite army to Gilgal, where Samuel had told Saul to wait for him. The Israelite army was facing a Philistine army, and Saul was supposed to stand in place for seven days, until Samuel arrived. Samuel planned to make whole-burnt offerings and sacrifices of well-being to GOD and then to share with Saul the guidance GOD would give him (1Sam 10:8).

Samuel did not arrive within the allotted seven days, and the Israelites began to slip away from Saul. So Saul offered the whole-burnt offering himself, and he also intended to make the sacrifice of well-being; however, Samuel arrived soon after Saul made the first offering. Samuel questioned Saul about his actions, and Saul said that he had "forced" himself to make the offering, because he had begun to feel vulnerable to attack (1Sam 13:12).

Samuel told Saul that he had acted foolishly. After all, it was Samuel who was going to give Saul his marching orders, and sacrifices Saul initiated would do no good. Saul had attempted to appropriate priestly authority to himself, a misstep whose folly the Book of Hebrews would later point out, as Samuel did (Heb 5:4). The LORD had made Saul king of Israel, but his sin was so grievous that He decreed that his reign would not continue (1Sam 13:14).

A military victory over the Amalekites led to Saul's second defiance of the LORD for the sake of sacrificial ritual. Samuel had told Saul that GOD wanted him to attack Amalek and to destroy all its people and animals (1Sam 15:3). Saul defeated the Amalekites, but instead of killing all the animals, he and the Israelites let the best of them live so that they might sacrifice them to GOD (1Sam 15:15). Thus, once again, Saul misjudged that sacrificial ritual took priority over obedience to GOD. In the following verses, Samuel captures the moral of Saul's story:

And Samuel said,
"Has the LORD as great delight in burnt offerings and sacrifices
as in obedience to the voice of the LORD?
Surely, to obey is better than sacrifice,
and to heed than the fat of rams.
For rebellion is no less a sin than divination,
and stubbornness is like iniquity and idolatry.
Because you have rejected the word of the LORD,
He has also rejected you from being king." (1Sam 15:22-23)

GOD desired the Israelites to sin less and, by implication, to sacrifice less. He desired obedience, not sacrifice.

This theme surfaces again in Psalm 40, where the psalmist writes that GOD saved him from a desolate pit and put a new song of praise in his mouth. Part of that song goes like this:

Sacrifice and offering you do not desire,
but you have given me an open ear.
Burnt offering and sin offering
you have not required.
Then I said, "Here I am:
in the scroll of the book it is written of me.
I delight to do your will, O my GOD;
your law is within my heart." (Ps 40:6-8)

The psalmist had learned the lesson that GOD taught via Saul's tale; and, in the second half of the passage above, Christ himself becomes the speaker and speaks of the New Covenant to come (Heb 10:5-9). Listening to GOD with "an open ear" and doing His will were more important than offering sacrifices. Rituals aren't necessary; true obedience originates "within my heart."

In Psalm 69, the psalmist recounts the humiliations he is suffering because of his faith in GOD. He has more haters than hairs on his head. He is accused falsely. He is the subject of gossip, and drunkards ridicule him in song. The psalmist prays to GOD to save him and to destroy his enemies. He sees his wished-for deliverance as a potential opportunity:

I will praise the name of GOD with a song;
I will magnify Him with thanksgiving.
This will please the LORD more than an ox
or a bull with horns and hoofs.
Let the oppressed see it and be glad;
you who seek GOD, let your hearts revive.
For the LORD hears the needy,
and does not despise His own that are in bonds. (Ps 69:30-33)

The psalmist perceives that he could accomplish more by singing songs of praise than he could by offering sacrifices. He implies that sacrifice should not be used as an excuse not to perform good works, just as it should not be used as a license to sin actively.

In the Book of Proverbs, GOD adds another voice to this chorus, with these verses:

All deeds are right in the sight of the doer,
but the LORD weighs the heart.
To do righteousness and justice
is more acceptable to the LORD than sacrifice. (Prov 21:2-3)

Again, no matter how fastidiously we might adhere to the details of GOD's law, GOD's primary interest always will lie in what we give of the heart. To do "righteousness and justice" is to give of the heart; to offer sacrifice was less assuredly so.

In the first chapter of the Book of Isaiah, GOD forcefully rejects the Israelites' sacrifices:

What to me is the multitude of your sacrifices?
says the LORD;
I have had enough of burnt offerings of rams
and the fat of fed beasts;
I do not delight in the blood of bulls,
or of lambs, or of goats.
When you come to appear before me, who asked this from your hand?
Trample my courts no more. (Isa 1:11-12)

GOD goes on to say that bringing offerings is futile and that the Israelites' hands are covered in blood. He commands the Israelites to cleanse themselves, to do good, and to seek justice. On top of that, His references to blood and the cleansing of it ought to have sounded an especially loud alarm among the Israelites. In the Book of Leviticus (Lev 17:11) and also in the Book of Genesis (Gen 9:4), GOD emphasizes that the life of the body is in its blood. He decrees that the shedding of human blood should be punished in kind (Gen 9:6), and that anyone who slaughters an animal without presenting it as an offering at the Tabernacle should be held guilty of bloodshed and banished (Lev 17:3-4).

GOD abhors the bloodthirsty (Ps 5:6), and He clearly made blood an important component of His Design. By invoking it in His dressing-down of the Israelites, He ratcheted up its severity. The Israelites had twisted the sacrificial rite into an exercise in bloodshed, into an insult to GOD. Better to abandon the practice altogether than to continue in that mode.

In the Book of Micah, Micah asks what he should present to the LORD and lists animal sacrifices as a possibility. He receives an answer from the LORD that He requires him only to be just, kind, and humble (Mic 6:6-8). A verse in the Book of Hosea reads, "For I desire steadfast love and not sacrifice, / the knowledge of GOD rather than burnt offerings" (Hos 6:6). Jesus himself made use of this verse during his ministry on earth, paraphrasing it as, "I desire mercy, not sacrifice" (Mt 9:13, 12:7-8).

Perfect Sacrifice. With his own sacrifice, Jesus sealed the case against animal sacrifice. The Book of Hebrews captures the futility of the practice:

But in these sacrifices there is a reminder of sin year after year. For it is impossible for the blood of bulls and goats to take away sins. (Heb 10:3-4)

Although the Epistle speaks the truth, GOD could not have made a mistake when He laid out for Moses His laws concerning sacrifice, on the momentous occasion of His appearance on Mount Sinai. Surely, in the end, whether we succeeded, miraculously, or failed in our efforts to effect right sacrifices, GOD's plan was for sacrificial rites to teach us the important lessons they have in fact taught us, lessons such as these: GOD will not be deceived by shows of faith that are not backed by heartfelt faith; our sinful nature can lead us to make a sin out of almost anything, including opportunities GOD gives us to cleanse ourselves of sin; GOD wants us to live according to the morals that the Bible tells us, in the verses cited above, were omitted from sacrificial rites as actually practiced – righteousness, justice, obedience, humility, love, mercy, kindness, and others. These are important lessons; they teach us about the nature of GOD and about our relationship with Him. Sacrificed animals played a central role in this, and so, paradoxically, despite our failures, GOD did not allow the animals to be sacrificed in vain.

Even before the time of Christ, GOD had tired of animal sacrifice, and He left it to us to study the Bible in search of the wisdom of His sacrificial law. GOD did not encourage sacrifice beyond the point where its lessons had been revealed to us. He did not call for animal sacrifice lightly. GOD values His animals, and the saga of animal sacrifice gives us another reason to value them as well.

5 ECONOMICS I

The Bible acknowledges animals' economic value, but, as noted in chapter 3, it also conveys the message that the value good people place on animals exceeds that value. Good people bring a spirit of caring to the various roles they play in animals' lives. In one episode, this spirit leads Saul to his first meeting with Samuel, and in another, it sets Rebekah on the path to her union with Isaac. Through the prophet Zechariah, GOD expresses His disapproval of people's elevating cash over caring. GOD also disapproves of people's idolizing animals, a practice that places too much value on them.

One need look no farther than the first three books of the Bible to find examples of animals' having economic value. In the Book of Genesis, Abraham is said to be "very rich in livestock" (Gen 13:2). The Book of Exodus lays out the price thieves had to pay for stealing animals (Ex 22:1-4): two animals for each stolen animal the thieves still had in their possession; more animals for each stolen animal they did not. Depending on what they could afford, the Book of Leviticus gives people options for the sin offerings they would present at the altar: a sheep if they could afford it; otherwise, two turtledoves or two pigeons; otherwise, some "choice flour" (Lev 5:6-11).

Saul and The Donkeys. The way Saul, the would-be king whose misguided sacrifices led to his downfall, first came to meet the prophet Samuel reinforces the biblical theme that animals are of more value than their economic value would imply. At the time, Saul still enjoyed GOD's favor. The donkeys of Saul's father had gone astray, and his father had asked Saul to look for them. Saul searched high and low for them:

He passed through the hill country of Ephraim and passed through the land of Shalisha, but he did not find them. And he passed through the land of Shaalim, but they were not there. Then he passed through the land of Benjamin, but he did not find them.
When he came to the land of Zuph, he said to the boy who was with him, "Let us turn back, or my father will stop worrying about the donkeys and worry about us." (1Sam 9:4-5)

Saul did not turn back, because the servant boy pointed him in the direction of Samuel, who lived nearby. They went to meet with Samuel, to see if he could shed light on why they had travelled so far (1Sam 9:6-10). GOD had commanded Samuel to make Saul king. Notwithstanding the importance of that assignment, Samuel acknowledged the donkeys:

Then Saul approached Samuel inside the gate, and said, "Tell me, please, where is the house of the seer?" Samuel answered Saul, "I am the seer; go up before me to the shrine, for today you shall eat with me, and in the morning I will let you go and will tell you all that is on your mind. As for your donkeys that were lost three days ago, give no further thought to them, for they have been found. And on whom is all Israel's desire fixed, if not on you and all your ancestral house?" (1Sam 9:18-20)

If the donkeys had been of no more value than their economic value, Samuel surely would have advised Saul not to dwell on such a trivial matter; it would have been unthinkable for Saul to worry about a little money when he was about to be anointed ruler of Israel, its very first king. Saul had travelled far in search of the donkeys, because he knew that his father was worried about them; and Samuel knew that Saul too was worried about them. Samuel did not consider Saul's concern to be unimportant. He took it seriously, and he eased Saul's mind by telling him that the donkeys had been found.

Rebekah and the Camels. In the Book of Genesis, Abraham dispatches a servant of his to find a bride for Isaac, his son (Gen 24:1-9). The servant stops at a well outside the city of Nahor and asks GOD to give him a sign. The women of Nahor were making their evening visits to the communal well, and the servant prayed that Isaac's future bride would be a woman who would give him a drink when he asked, and who also would offer to water his camels (Gen 24:14). Rebekah showed up at the well, gave the servant a drink, and then said, "I will draw for your camels also, until they have finished drinking" (Gen 24:19).

Isaac and Rebekah were married and begot two sons, Esau and Jacob. Isaac, whom GOD eventually blinded, favored Esau, whom GOD came to despise (Gen 25:28). Rebekah favored Jacob, whom GOD eventually renamed Israel, making him the namesake of His chosen people (Gen 35:10). So, in a sense, the inception of the nation of Israel can be traced to a young woman's show of kindness to a stranger's camels, a clear endorsement of such kindness, which does not concern itself with cash value.

Zechariah and the Flock. Finally, in a passage in the Book of Zechariah, the evil of exploiting animals rises to the surface. In this passage, shepherds symbolize leaders and sheep symbolize the people:

Thus said the LORD my GOD: Be a shepherd of the flock doomed to slaughter. Those who buy them kill them and go unpunished; and those who sell them say, "Blessed be the LORD, for I have become rich;" and their own shepherds have no pity on them. (Zech 11:4-5)

This analogy is founded on a divine expectation that shepherds have pity on their flocks and that they not abandon them to exploitation. Animals have economic value, but they count for more than money. The Bible anticipates that we readers will know this with its stories like Saul's, in which caring about animals is people's natural way. And the Bible expects us to know that certain ways of treating animals can be metaphors for the exploitation of people, because the treatment is exploitative at the level of the animals themselves. In sum, it is more important for us to care about animals than about our pocketbooks.

Idolaters and the Animals. In one way animals are worthless, and that is as the idols people have made of them through the ages. Many of the idols that the Bible describes take the form of animals. Aaron led the Israelites to make the golden calf because Moses was delayed in coming down from Mount Sinai (Ex 32:4); they made it even though GOD already had given them the Ten Commandments, the second of which is not to make idols. King Jeroboam made two golden calves to lure the Israelites away from GOD with them (1Kings 12:28). The Israelites even permitted themselves to idolize the bronze serpent Moses made in the desert, to heal the snakebitten people with it (Num 21:5-9). As a result, King Hezekiah had to destroy it (2Kings 18:4), in an act that deprived all succeeding generations of an interesting historical artifact.

The Bible directs intolerant words toward animal idols. Of idolaters and their idols, the prophet Hosea remarks, "People are kissing calves!" (Hos 13:2). In the Book of Deuteronomy, Moses tells of destroying the golden calf, which he calls "the sinful thing." He says that he "burned it with fire and crushed it, grinding it thoroughly, until it was reduced to dust; and I threw the dust of it into the stream that runs down the mountain" (Deut 9:21).

In one of his visions, the prophet Ezekiel observes the desecration of the Temple:

He said to me, "Go in, and see the vile abominations that they are committing here." So I went in and looked; there, portrayed on the wall all around, were all kinds of creeping things, and loathsome animals, and all the idols of the house of Israel. (Ezek 8:9-10)

Such harsh words are inspired by idols and idolatry, and not by animals themselves. Animals are not to blame for idolaters' choosing to model their false gods on them. On the contrary, in the following verse, Isaiah imagines animals as victims of a kind:

Bel bows down, Nebo stoops,
their idols are on beasts and cattle;
these things you carry are loaded
as burdens on weary animals. (Isa 46:1)

Here, idols are burdens on animals, just as they are a burden on GOD and on idolaters themselves, even if they do not realize it. We should value animals, but we should not overvalue them, as idols. They should be objects of mercy and not objects of worship.

6 FAITH IN ECCLESIASTES

At times, the Bible challenges us to ponder our own destinies by comparing or contrasting them with animals'. GOD incorporates such a challenge into the Book of Ecclesiastes, a challenge that, as the book progresses, has the effect not of weakening our faith but of strengthening it. Here is the challenging passage:

I said in my heart with regard to human beings that GOD is testing them to show that they are but animals. For the fate of humans and the fate of animals is the same; as one dies, so dies the other. They all have the same breath, and humans have no advantage over the animals; for all is vanity. All go to one place; all are from the dust, and all turn to dust again. Who knows whether the human spirit goes upward and the spirit of animals goes downward to the earth? So I saw that there is nothing better than that all should enjoy their work, for that is their lot; who can bring them to see what will be after them? (Ecc 3:18-22)

This passage, presently referred to as the "test passage," should not be misinterpreted as an assertion of truth – it is not. The test passage is a test, a test of the proposition that we are "but animals." Its first sentence introduces it as a test, and much of the rest of it presents ostensibly supporting arguments. Its conclusions compel us to choose between reason and faith. Solomon develops two themes in Ecclesiastes that help us with our choice: the theme that human understanding is limited and, intriguingly, the theme that only through faith can we enjoy our work.

If it were true, the test passage would undermine two of the Bible's core teachings. First, the notion that our spirits might be on a level with or even subordinate to animals' spirits defies the very first chapters of the Book of Genesis. We were made in GOD's image, and we were given dominion over the animals; GOD even presented the animals to Adam to be given their names (Gen 2:19).

Second, in one of the test passage's verses, Solomon observes that both humans and animals arise from and return to dust; and in the verse that follows, Solomon seems to infer that this bears on our spiritual fate. However, elsewhere, the Bible draws a line between earthly considerations and spiritual considerations. The shared fate of humans' and animals' earthly bodies has no bearing on our respective spiritual destinies. GOD has built this distinction into His Design; it is a cornerstone of the Christian faith. The test passage cries out to be scrutinized; its dissonance with other biblical passages demands that we give it a careful hearing.

Reason. In Ecclesiastes, Solomon points out the limitations of human understanding, and in the test passage's battle between faith and reason, those limitations cripple the case for the latter. In chapter 8, Solomon points out that we cannot comprehend GOD's design work

Then I saw all the work of GOD, that no one can find out what is happening under the sun. However much they may toil in seeking, they will not find it out; even though those who are wise claim to know, they cannot find it out. (Ecc 8:17)

Verses 3:10-11 buttress this, and in chapter 7, Solomon comments on the limitations of his own wisdom:

All this I have tested by wisdom; I said, "I will be wise," but it was far from me. That which is is far off, and deep, very deep; who can find it out? (Ecc 7:23-24)

No one can find it out; at some point, human understanding inevitably fails. If the test passage's arguments convince us, they also deceive us, and we choose wisely by questioning our own wisdom. Questioning it sometimes splashes us with the cold reality of its insufficiency and awakens us to the possibilities of faith.

Faith. Throughout Ecclesiastes, at the same time Solomon is assailing the test passage's reliance on flawed, human reasoning, he is advancing the case for faith. In the test passage, Solomon commends faith to us, subtly, with his statement, "So I saw that there is nothing better than that all should enjoy their work." Elsewhere in Ecclesiastes, Solomon advises us to apply ourselves to our work (Ecc 9:10), and he links our enjoyment of it to GOD's presence in our lives. He writes that it is a gift from GOD for us to enjoy our work (Ecc 5:19) and that apart from GOD, we cannot enjoy it (Ecc 2:24-25).

So, when he extols the enjoyment of work near the end of the test passage, Solomon is calling us to invite GOD into our lives – that is, to put our faith in Him. In this way, as the test passage draws to a close, faith triumphs over reason, and the biblical story of Creation remains intact. We retain our superiority over animals, while the animals help GOD, in Ecclesiastes, to strengthen our faith.

7 SPIRIT

While they do not pretend to address the particulars of the animals' place in the spiritual realm, Ecclesiastes and one of the Psalms, Psalm 49, do imply that human death and animal death differ in nature. However, despite that revelation, the Bible contains a number of passages that point to an animal spirituality of some kind. If GOD has not revealed the exact nature of that spirituality to us, His reticence gives us another opportunity to strengthen our faith, and it might be sending us a message concerning how He expects us to treat animals.

The Soul of a Dove. In chapter 6 and in chapter 1, some of the biblical excerpts have associated spirit with animals. For example, in chapter 6's "test passage," from Ecclesiastes (Ecc 3:18-22), Solomon alludes to the "spirit of animals." That allusion is not an element of the "test" per se; it draws less attention to itself than does the suggestion that the human spirit can scarcely be distinguished from the animal spirit. When Solomon challenges us by comparing the human spirit to the animal spirit, he is comparing it to something real and not to something imagined.

In Psalm 104, the Spirit of GOD brings animals into being:

When You send forth Your Spirit, they are created;
and You renew the face of the ground (Ps 104:30).

Psalm 74 uses an animal's soul to symbolize GOD's people:

Do not deliver the soul of Your dove to the wild animals;
do not forget the life of Your poor forever. (Ps 74:19)

All of these verses explicitly associate spirit with animals. Other passages imply an association, in that they make the most sense in a context of animal spirituality.

Breath. In Ecclesiastes, as Solomon reflects on the similarities between humans and animals, he relates that "they all have the same breath." This particular statement finds support elsewhere in the Bible. The "breath" connotes a life force, a fundamental endowment of both humans and animals that sets them apart from the rest of Creation. The Book of Genesis introduces the breath of life in its account of Adam's creation:

Then the LORD GOD formed man from the dust of the ground, and breathed into his nostrils the breath of life; and the man became a living being (Gen 2:7).

Later in Genesis, the breath of life is located in animals, as well as in humans:

And all flesh died that moved on the earth, birds, domestic animals, wild animals, all swarming creatures that swarm on the earth, and all human beings; everything on dry land in whose nostrils was the breath of life died (Gen 7:21-22).

Finally, in the Book of Job, Elihu makes the following statement regarding GOD, GOD's Spirit, and GOD's breath:

If He should take back His Spirit to Himself
and gather to Himself His breath,
all flesh would perish together,
and all mortals return to dust (Job 34:14-15).

Here, the breath of life is portrayed as GOD's breath, and, in combination with the other quotations above, that portrayal makes a clear connection between animals and spirit. GOD's breath, the breath of life, is undeniably spiritual in nature: it comes directly from GOD Himself, and it works wonders that nothing other than Spirit can work. It requires divine power to create a living being from dust, and GOD's breath of life carries with it that power. The breath of life transcends dust; it imbues dust with Spirit, to produce the miracle that is life.

Blood. Chapter 2 mentions GOD's extraordinary death sentence for any animal that tread on Mount Sinai during His appearances to Moses there (Ex 19:12-13). While that command was an exception rather than the rule, it hints at a minimal moral expectation of animals, and moral expectations belong to the spiritual realm. The Bible contains a few other hints as well.

First of all, the Book of Leviticus lays down the following law:

The man who lies with his father's wife has uncovered his father's nakedness; both of them shall be put to death; their blood is upon them. If a man lies with his daughter-in-law, both of them shall be put to death; they have committed perversion, their blood is upon them. If a man lies with a male as with a woman, both of them have committed an abomination; they shall be put to death; their blood is upon them. If a man takes a wife and her mother also, it is depravity; they shall be burned to death, both he and they, that there may be no depravity among you. If a man has sexual relations with an animal, he shall be put to death; and you shall kill the animal. If a woman approaches any animal and has sexual relations with it, you shall kill the woman and the animal; they shall be put to death, their blood is upon them. (Lev 20:11-16)

In this passage, the fraught refrain "their blood is upon them" is meant to indicate that the offenders themselves, and not their executioners, would be to blame for their deaths. The statement is applied both to humans and to animals, implying that the offending animals would bear a measure of responsibility for their wrongdoing, like the Mount Sinai animals. Bearing responsibility is a moral matter, and therefore a spiritual matter. It is spirit that allows us to tell right from wrong, and by holding animals responsible for certain egregious wrongs, the Bible points toward an animal spirituality.

   Connections. In the Book of Genesis, upon making His covenant with Noah and the animals never to flood the earth again (Gen 9:8-11), GOD established the rainbow as a reminder of it, for Himself:

"When the bow is in the clouds, I will see it and remember the everlasting covenant between GOD and every living creature of all flesh that is on the earth." GOD said to Noah, "This is the sign of the covenant that I have established between Me and all flesh that is on the earth." (Gen 9:16-17)

So, GOD not only thinks of us when He sees the rainbow, but He also thinks of the animals. In addition to relating the story of the Bow Covenant, the Bible tells of other, less formal communications between GOD and animals – communications in both directions. The Bible leaves it to us to judge whether any of these interactions point to an animal spirituality; it does not state explicitly that they do. As noted in chapter 1, in the Book of Joel, the wild animals cry to GOD for lack of water (Joel 1:20). In the Book of Isaiah, GOD relates that the wild animals – even the ill-tempered jackals and ostriches -- will honor Him when He fulfills a promise to produce water in the wilderness and rivers in the desert (Isa 43:20). In the Book of Jonah, GOD "spoke to" the fish, telling it to disgorge Jonah (Jonah 2:10). In his Epistle to the Colossians, Paul notes that the animals received the Good News of the Gospel:

And you who were once estranged and hostile in mind, doing evil deeds, he has now reconciled in his fleshly body through death, so as to present you holy and blameless and irreproachable before Him – provided that you continue securely established and steadfast in the faith, without shifting from the hope promised by the Gospel that you heard, which has been proclaimed to every creature under heaven. I, Paul, became a servant of this Gospel. (Col 1:21-23).

In the Book of Revelation, the animals celebrate this Gospel:

Then I heard every creature in heaven and on earth and under the earth and in the sea and all that is in them, singing,
"To the one seated on the throne and to the Lamb
be blessing and honor and glory and might
forever and ever!"
And the four living creatures said, "Amen!" And the elders fell down and worshipped. (Rev 5:13-14).

Thus, the animals will proclaim the Good News themselves that was proclaimed to them.

   GOD speaks to animals directly, and they to Him. The animals share in the Gospel and ultimately will share of it. Christians who take these as signs of an animal spirituality are on sound footing, especially in light of the other signs the Bible gives us – GOD's covenant with the animals, the animals' "breath of life," moral expectations of animals, and direct references to an animal spirit. If animals are spiritual in nature, then some sort of animal afterlife arises as a possibility – and that possibility spawns further possibilities for our spiritual growth.

   Afterlife. The possibilities for us relate respectively to what we do not control and to what we do control vis-a-vis the animals. The former presents us with another opportunity to strengthen our faith; the latter, to manifest our faith through prayer.

   GOD holds the fate of the animals in His hands. While we hold dominion over the animals, our powers pale in comparison to the powers of their Creator. GOD has the power to establish the animals' place in His spiritual hierarchy; we do not. In Psalm 49, which likens the pompous rich to "the animals that perish," GOD makes it clear that there is a finality to animals' deaths. However, He also has made the existence of animal spirit nearly as certain to us, and the animals appear, singing, at the Apocalypse. With GOD, it is not impossible that these seemingly incompatible messages truly reflect His Design.

Perhaps any animal afterlife takes on a different nature from ours. Perhaps animals have an afterlife that is tied to the Book of Revelation's four attendants to the throne, alluded to above and further described below:

and in front of the throne there is something like a sea of glass, like crystal. Around the throne, and on each side of the throne, are four living creatures, full of eyes in front and behind: the first living creature like a lion, the second living creature like an ox, the third living creature with a face like a human face, and the fourth living creature like a flying eagle. And the four living creatures, each of them with six wings, are full of eyes all around and inside. Day and night without ceasing they sing,
"Holy, holy, holy,
the LORD GOD the Almighty,
who was and is and is to come." (Rev 4:6-8)

Isaiah also wrote of these creatures, or seraphs, and transcribed the lyrics of their song (Isa 6:2-3). Furthermore, the seraphs appear in the Book of Ezekiel. In his vision, Ezekiel also sees four wheels, one for each of the seraphs:

When the living creatures moved, the wheels moved beside them; and when the living creatures rose from the earth, the wheels rose. Wherever the spirit would go, they went, and the wheels rose along with them; for the spirit of the living creatures was in the wheels. (Ezek 1:19-20)

All of these visions – Isaiah's; Ezekiel's; and John's, in the Book of Revelation – contain some tantalizing suggestions but remain mysterious. The four seraphs sing GOD's praises, as do all of GOD's creatures; and the seraphs say "Amen" to the song that all the other creatures sing. Thus, the seraphs are connected to animals and also to spirit, which Ezekiel tells us is "in the wheels."

All else aside, perhaps GOD wants to reemphasize with these suggestive visions that we have no choice but to yield to His will concerning animals in the afterlife, and that we might do well to approach the visions in the spirit of another of the Psalms, Psalm 131:

O LORD, my heart is not lifted up,
my eyes are not raised too high;
I do not occupy myself with things
too great and too marvelous for me. (Ps 131:1)

With this sentiment, the Bible has brought us full circle to a theme of Ecclesiastes, inviting us again to put our faith in GOD and to trust that His goodness will prevail. The animals are fundamentally His. They are an element of His Creation, an element of His Design, and an element of His Plan. If we commend to Him what we cannot control, He will unburden us of it and allow us to attend to what we can.

Prayer. We may pray for the animals, but it would be hypocritical of us to pray for them without first examining our own treatment of them. GOD has made them subordinate to us; we have much power over them. We would undermine His trust in us if we neglected to attend to our own responsibilities before we asked Him to make commitments to us on their behalf. If the animals present a genuine opportunity for us to show mercy, then we ought to show them mercy. If the animals present a genuine opportunity for us to be gracious, then we ought to be gracious toward them. If the animals present a genuine opportunity for us to love, then we ought to love them. Let us be guided by these morals and other morals as we move forward in our priceless relationship with GOD's animals.

PART II

CHRIST'S ANIMALS

8 CHRIST'S WORDS

Jesus incorporated animals into many of his parables and other teachings, and like his Father's, Jesus's words sometimes allude to animals' appealing traits and sometimes to their unappealing traits. But Jesus never attacks the animals; rather, he accepts them as they are. At Jesus's baptism, the peace-giving Holy Spirit, who plays such a pivotal role in the New Testament, is depicted as a dove, and that depiction echoes throughout the Bible, to profound effect. Finally, the Gospels sometimes draw comparisons between Jesus and animals, and the comparisons highlight his humble nature.

By Jesus. A sample of some of Jesus's teachings illustrates what a big part animals play in them...

The scribes and Pharisees are "snakes" and "vipers" (Mt 23:33). They are blind guides, straining out gnats but swallowing camels (Mt 23:24). Herod is a cunning "fox" (Lk 13:32).

"It is easier for a camel to go through the eye of a needle than for someone who is rich to enter the kingdom of GOD" (Mk 10:25).

Lazarus was so downtrodden that even the dogs treated him with contempt, gathering around to lick his sores (Lk 16:21).

The list goes on. Again, in these examples, Jesus does not judge animals; he uses their traits and behaviors to make points about people with them. Even though vipers are a danger to people, Jesus does not expect them to be any different; he directs his anger at the Pharisees, who pose a danger to people but should not.

In at least one instance, Jesus encourages behavior that, in the context of the animal world, signals danger. He gives his Disciples these words of wisdom as he prepares them to spread his message on their own: "See, I am sending you out like sheep into the midst of wolves; so be wise as serpents and innocent as doves" (Mt 10:16). This passage shows again that Jesus accepted animals' innocuous traits and animals' dangerous traits alike, going so far as to advise his Disciples to take on one of the latter, the calculating wisdom of serpents.

Dove of Peace. Christians know from firsthand experience that to be at peace is to live according to GOD's will; Paul shares his knowledge of this in his Epistle to the Romans (Rom 8:5-9). Through expressions of GOD's will, the Holy Spirit serves as a guidepost to peace. In the Gospels, the Holy Spirit first appears at Christ's baptism:

And when Jesus had been baptized, just as he came up from the water, suddenly the heavens were opened to him and he saw the Spirit of GOD descending like a dove and alighting on him. And a voice from heaven said, "This is my Son, the Beloved, with whom I am well pleased." (Mt 3:16-17)

The image of the dove naturally recalls the dove that returned to Noah with an olive leaf in its beak, a sign that, by His grace, GOD had allowed the floodwaters to recede and was prepared to renew his relationship with the human race (Gen 8:8-12). Like that dove, the Holy Spirit heralded a new covenant, but in the Spirit's case, the Covenant involves the ultimate forgiveness and the eternal peace to be found in Jesus.

By choosing the words "alighting on" to describe the Spirit's filling Jesus, Matthew recalls prophecies like the prophecy below. Isaiah wrote this prophecy, and Jesus read it aloud at a Sabbath service in a Nazarene synagogue:

The Spirit of the LORD is upon me,
because he has anointed me
to bring good news to the poor.
He has sent me to proclaim release to the captives
and recovery of sight to the blind,
to let the oppressed go free,
to proclaim the year of the LORD 's favor. (Lk 4:18-19)

Matthew's avian description resonates with Isaiah's, and whether it is expressed as the Spirit of the LORD being "upon me" or as the Spirit of GOD "alighting on him," the message is the same: the Messiah was baptized in the Holy Spirit, the Dove. Accordingly, in the synagogue, Jesus identified himself as the subject of Isaiah's prophecy.

Chapter 11 of the Book of Isaiah includes language similar to the opening of the prophecy Jesus read; the second verse of that chapter begins, "The Spirit of the LORD shall rest on him." Later in the chapter, animals help to depict the peaceful age the New Covenant will usher in:

The wolf shall live with the lamb,
the leopard shall lie down with the kid,
the calf and the lion and the fatling together,
and a little child shall lead them.
The cow and the bear shall graze,
their young shall lie down together,
and the lion shall eat straw like the ox.
The nursing child shall play over the hole of the asp,
and the weaned child shall put his hand on the adder's den.
They will not hurt or destroy on all My holy mountain;
for the earth will be full of the knowledge of the LORD
as the waters cover the sea. (Isa 11:6-9)

In this prophecy, with the animals' help, Isaiah foretells a return to an Edenic state, a time before predator and prey (Gen 1:30), a time before enmity between human and serpent (Gen 3:15), and a time without sin and of harmony with GOD.

Christ's baptism was a momentous event at which all three Persons of the Trinity made prominent appearances. Featuring the Holy Spirit as a dove, which has become a symbol of peace, Matthew's account of the baptism reverberates through the Bible. The Dove carries us back to the time of Noah and the Bow Covenant, which was the first covenant GOD made with all of humankind; and Jesus soon would seal the New Covenant, which is the final covenant. The Dove also carries us back to Isaiah, whose prophecies carry us forward to that New Covenant, which, in turn, is reminiscent of peaceful Eden; the wolf and the lamb, the leopard and the kid, and the others help to make the New Covenant's perfect peace tangible to us.

Of Jesus. After the baptism, the Holy Spirit inspired Jesus to go forth into the wilderness, where he would fast for forty days and endure Satan's temptations. In his account of the episode, Mark introduces a common theme in the comparisons the Bible makes between Jesus and the animals: the comparisons speak to Jesus's humility. Mark's account includes the detail that when he was in the wilderness, Jesus was "with the wild beasts" – in contrast to his having been, not long before, in view of the heavens' opening above him. This implies that Jesus emerged from his baptism not haughty, but humble. He did not object to the Holy Spirit's counsel; rather, he embraced it and ventured – at peace with GOD, to be sure – into the domain of the wild beasts.

When a repentant scribe told Jesus that he would follow him wherever he went, Jesus replied, "Foxes have holes, and birds of the air have nests; but the Son of Man has nowhere to lay his head" (Mt 8:20). On one level, with this reply, Jesus lovingly impressed upon the scribe that the uncertain, itinerant life, the life for which Jesus had specially chosen his Apostles, does not suit everyone; during his time on earth, Jesus could not provide his followers with the comforts of home. On the other hand, Jesus's response implies that by virtue of His providing homes to birds and foxes, GOD would not begrudge the comforts of home to people. In another exchange, when the Gerasene demoniac, from whom Jesus expelled a "legion" of demons, begged Jesus to take him along, Jesus said to him, "Return to your home, and declare how much GOD has done for you" (Lk 8:39). Jesus delivered a similar message to the repentant scribe, with the implied assurance that GOD would have wanted him to have a home.

On another level, Jesus's statement implies that Jesus was so humble and so unassuming that he would choose to serve us even though he felt less at home here than animals do. In the Gospel of John, as Jesus prays on the day of his arrest, he emphasizes that his followers do not belong to the world (Jn 17:14-18). In the Book of Hebrews, it is written that holy people of the Old Testament longed for their heavenly home and thought of themselves as foreigners and strangers in this world (Heb 11:13-16). Animals help to cast Jesus, who had nowhere to lay his head, in the same light and to give some expression to the bottomless depths of his humility.

In the House of the Father. The day after his Triumphal Entry into Jerusalem and his disruption of the Temple, Jesus returned to the Temple (Mt 21:23). Throughout the day, he was questioned by the chief priests, the elders, the Pharisees, the Herodians, and the Sadducees. Despite this rude treatment, Jesus closed his day in the Temple with the following words:

"Jerusalem, Jerusalem, the city that kills the prophets and stones those who are sent to it! How often have I desired to gather your children together as a hen gathers her brood under her wings, and you were not willing! See, your house is left to you, desolate. For I tell you, you will not see me again until you say, 'Blessed is the one who comes in the name of the LORD.'" (Mt 23:37-39)

In this passage, the image of the hen gives us still another window onto Jesus's boundless humility. Having been received inhospitably into his own Father's House, Jesus expressed love for his ungracious hosts, comparing himself to a protective and nurturing animal.

Comparisons like this are stated or implied elsewhere in the New Testament, especially in connection with Jesus's sacrifice. The Lamb of GOD, the newborn Jesus was laid down in a manger, a feeding trough for livestock (Lk 2:7). While the Old Covenant forbade the consumption of animal blood (Deut 12:23), Jesus proffered his own blood, in the form of wine, at the Last Supper (Mk 14:24). Whereas GOD led a ram to act as a sacrificial surrogate for Isaac (Gen 22:13), He made no such provision for His own Son. Like a sacrificial lamb, Jesus went silently to his death; unlike a sacrificial lamb, he had foreknowledge of his death (Lk 9:22), he sweat blood on the eve of it (Lk 22:44), and he was tortured to death, over a protracted period.

Although the animals thus enhance the Gospels' narratives of Jesus's earthly life, segments of the writings of two of Jesus's Apostles, Paul and Peter, might seem, at first glance, to pass unfavorable judgments on animals. But a closer look reveals that these holy men honored the accepting spirit of Jesus's teachings and of the Gospels on the whole.

9 THE MUZZLED OX

In his first Epistle to the Corinthians, the Apostle Paul makes a statement that calls GOD's concern for animals into question. In the Epistle, Paul defends his decision to work as a craftsman (Acts 18:1-3) instead of earning his living through the work of his ministry. Paul writes that he had a right to support himself with his ministerial work, but that taking payments would have made him beholden to persons other than the LORD. Even though Paul chose not to seek material gain from his ministry, he made the following defense of his right to do so:

For it is written in the law of Moses, "You shall not muzzle an ox while it is treading out grain." Is it for oxen that GOD is concerned? Or does He not speak entirely for our sake? It was indeed written for our sake, for whoever plows should plow in hope and whoever threshes should thresh in hope of a share in the crop. If we have sown spiritual good among you, is it too much if we reap your material benefits? (1Cor 9:9-11)

The verse Paul quotes is verse Deuteronomy 25:4. It appears in the Book of Deuteronomy among laws such as the law that needy laborers be paid daily (Deut 24:15) and the law that, under certain circumstances, the brother of a deceased man marry his widow (Deut 25:5). Deuteronomy 25:4 is symbolic of working people and their right to payment, a right that Jesus reaffirmed (Lk 10:7). The entire passage from Paul's Epistle could be taken as a sign that GOD never is concerned for oxen. However, other Bible verses indicate that GOD, and Jesus, are mindful of oxen, and also, in all likelihood, verse Deuteronomy 25:4 itself is built on a presumption of kindness toward animals.

Other Oxen. First, there are the Bible verses, including verses previously mentioned in *The Value of Animals*, that show that GOD does care for oxen and other animals: verses such as Genesis 9:10, which expressly applies the Bow Covenant to the domestic animals; Exodus 23:12, which calls for oxen to be rested on the Sabbath; and Psalm 145:9, which states that GOD's compassion is over all of His Creation.

In the following extended metaphor, Jesus exhibits a sensitivity to the demands placed on draft animals:

"Come to me, all you that are weary and are carrying heavy burdens, and I will give you rest. Take my yoke upon you, and learn from me; for I am gentle and humble in heart, and you will find rest for your souls. For my yoke is easy, and my burden is light." (Mt 11:28-30)

In the main, Jesus is inviting his listeners to take comfort in him; but the wording of his invitation evinces a sensitivity to animals' workloads. He distinguishes between heavy burdens and light, and between the wearisome and the restful. These distinctions relate to the world of animals, and, in this analogy, Jesus applies them to the world of us humans. At a minimum, oxen did not escape Jesus's notice; not unlikely, the overburdening of animals did not escape Jesus's reproach.

Literal, Symbol. Paul's comments about verse Deuteronomy 25:4 make it clear that the verse is purely symbolic and was not written for the benefit of oxen. Irrespective of that, the verse might tell a tale of mercy toward animals, anyway.

Even though few of us in the developed world work with oxen these days, even that set of us can see the kindness in a custom not to muzzle oxen while they are treading out grain. It would be unkind to prevent them, by means of a muzzle, from eating some grain during their breaks for rest. Their hard work would make them hungry, and it would be cruel not to let them satisfy their hunger, with plenty of grain about.

If it did not make sense to us that the oxen should not be muzzled, then we would be left to wonder why GOD put the verse in the Bible. We would not understand what the verse symbolized, as we would not understand the verse at all. But we do understand what the verse means at the literal level, the level of oxen, and we also understand why the verse matters at that level. As a consequence, it is easy for us to see that the ox symbolizes a human worker and the grain symbolizes the worker's wages, as Paul points out.

The advice at the level of oxen probably was advice that righteous Israelites followed all along. Because the righteous know their animals' needs (Prov 12:10), it is likely that many Israelite farmers never did muzzle their oxen when the oxen were treading out grain. If, in fact, they did not, then Israelites like Paul would have looked for the symbolism in verse Deuteronomy 25:4 right away; it would have seemed obvious to them that GOD would not have put the guidance in the Bible unless it had some deeper meaning.

Moral. GOD has left it to us to make decisions such as whether to muzzle oxen, trusting us to make moral choices. Righteous Israelites would have set the muzzles aside. Because that practice makes sense to us, GOD can use verse Deuteronomy 25:4 to tell us symbolically with it how we should treat human workers. So, instead of being a putdown to animals, the verse emerges as one of the many that show that righteous people have caring relationships with animals. The presumption of caring relationships would have given Paul leave to dismiss as redundant, as a given, the verse's literal meaning, in favor of its true, symbolic meaning.

Is it for oxen that GOD is concerned? Not by way of verse Deuteronomy 25:4 – Paul explains that. But GOD enlists oxen to perform double duty here, and we may be grateful for that. First, the oxen help GOD to teach us the importance of treating human workers fairly. Second, they help Paul to express his determination not to allow his ministry to come under the influence of unscrupulous donors. That constitutes a core teaching of First Corinthians, chapter 9, and the animals play a role in support of it.

10 SECOND PETER, CHAPTER 2

In a passage from his second Epistle, Second Peter 2:9-13, the Apostle Peter might seem to us to harbor some hostility toward animals. He describes them in uncharitable terms, but other books of the Bible provide context that bears upon Peter's writing. Surely, Peter did not feel hostile toward all animals all of the time; in fact, when he wrote the passage, he most likely had only a single, small subclass of animals in mind. This interpretation finds support in the words of Christ himself. Thus, we should not interpret the passage as an attack on animals; it is not. The passage alerts us to the dangers posed by false prophets (2Pet 2:1), whom Peter compares to animals. We would miss the point if we misconstrued it to be a statement on animals' place in GOD's Design.

Here is the passage, in context:

For if GOD did not spare the angels when they sinned, but cast them into hell and committed them to chains of deepest darkness to be kept until the judgment; and if He did not spare the ancient world, even though He saved Noah, a herald of righteousness, with seven others, when He brought a flood on a world of the ungodly; and if by turning the cities of Sodom and Gomorrah to ashes He condemned them to extinction and made them an example of what is coming to the ungodly; and if He rescued Lot, a righteous man greatly distressed by the licentiousness of the lawless (for that righteous man, living among them day after day, was tormented in his righteous soul by their lawless deeds that he saw and heard), then the LORD knows how to rescue the godly from trial, and to keep the unrighteous under punishment until the day of judgment – especially those who indulge their flesh in depraved lust, and who despise authority.
Bold and willful, they are not afraid to slander the glorious ones, whereas angels, though greater in might and power, do not bring against them a slanderous judgment from the LORD. These people, however, are like irrational animals, mere creatures of instinct, born to be caught and killed. They slander what they do not understand, and when those creatures are destroyed, they also will be destroyed, suffering the penalty for doing wrong. They count it a pleasure to revel in the daytime. They are blots and blemishes, reveling in their dissipation while they feast with you. (2Pet 2:4-13)

In this passage, Peter likens false prophets to animals that he characterizes as "irrational animals, mere creatures of instinct, born to be caught and killed." He also relates that these animals ultimately will be destroyed and that the false prophets will be destroyed with them, on account of their sins.

Irrational Animals. Animals' irrational nature surfaces in Bible passages outside of chapter 2 of Second Peter, for example in Psalm 32:

I will instruct you and teach you the way you should go;
I will counsel you with my eye upon you.
Do not be like a horse or a mule, without understanding,
whose temper must be curbed with bit and bridle,
else it will not stay near you. (Ps 32:8-9)

People are supposed to be smarter than animals, and they should behave accordingly. GOD designed animals not to possess human understanding, and He points out their cognitive limitations in the Bible whenever it suits Him. He does not fault them for their limitations; rather, paradoxically, He invokes them to teach us lessons with them. In the Book of Jeremiah, GOD even rates an incorrigible Israel's level of knowledge lower than that possessed by migratory birds (Jer 8:7). In the passage from Second Peter, He directs His anger at the false prophets, whom He would expect to act in a rational manner, not in the irrational manner of animals.

Mere Creatures of Instinct. After Peter labels animals irrational, he proceeds to describe them as being "mere creatures of instinct." In the Book of Jude, the language of which Second Peter's echoes, Jude writes the following of certain ungodly intruders upon the early church, "But these people slander whatever they do not understand, and they are destroyed by those things that, like irrational animals, they know by instinct. Woe to them! For they go the way of Cain, and abandon themselves to Balaam's error for the sake of gain, and perish in Korah's rebellion" (Jude 10-11). Jude takes a neutral tone toward animals' instinctual knowledge; he saves his foreboding words for his subjects' reliance on such knowledge. Peter, on the other hand, with his phrase "mere creatures of instinct," seems to imply that animals are somehow contemptible; if animals are "mere" creatures, then they hardly merit our concern. But Peter's use of the word "mere" also gives us reason to ask whether he has some particular animals in mind and does not intend his descriptions to apply to all animals; his angry tone does not comport with the Bible's overall tone, including Jude's, of equanimity toward animals.

Peter would have embraced the truth of these verses, from the Book of Proverbs:

Four things on earth are small,
yet they are exceedingly wise:
the ants are a people without strength,
yet they provide their food in the summer;
the badgers are a people without power,
yet they make their homes in the rocks;
the locusts have no king,
yet all of them march in rank;
the lizard can be grasped in the hand,
yet it is found in kings' palaces. (Prov 30:24-28)

Peter certainly would not have dismissed these animals as "merely" instinctual beings; like us, he would have seen and appreciated the wisdom of their ways. Even if their behavior is fully or partly instinctual, Peter would have valued them for the role they play as GOD's messengers. He would not have sneered at GOD's having chosen to cast these animals in a favorable light; he was a man of faith, and with little doubt, he would have approached these verses with an attitude of openness and humility. The Bible's prevailing, unperturbed regard for animals, limitations and all, would not have eluded him.

Feed the Flock. In his first Epistle, Peter demonstrates that he values animals. In the following passage, he makes use of the comparison that appears so frequently in the Bible, the comparison that likens church leaders to shepherds and church members to sheep:

Now as an elder myself and a witness of the sufferings of Christ, as well as one who shares in the glory to be revealed, I exhort the elders among you to tend the flock of GOD that is in your charge, exercising the oversight, not under compulsion but willingly, as GOD would have you do it – not for sordid gain, but eagerly. Do not lord it over those in your charge, but be examples to the flock. And when the Chief Shepherd appears, you will win the crown of glory that never fades away. (1Pet 5:1-4)

Underlying these verses is the conviction – Peter's inspired conviction – that sheep are something more than "mere creatures of instinct." Knowing that sheep are worthy of their shepherds' best efforts to care for them, Peter knew that the sheep-and-shepherd analogy would have the effect he desired; he knew that he could use the analogy to convey the message that church members are worthy of church leaders' best efforts to care for them as well.

Born to be Caught and Killed. So, Peter's use of the sheep-and-shepherd analogy illustrates that he did not relegate all animals to the domain of "mere creatures of instinct." In fact, he seems to have relegated few of them to that domain. By describing the animals he has in mind as having been "born to be caught and killed," Peter eliminates almost all animals from consideration. Certainly, he eliminates domestic animals, which, by and large, only occasionally have to be captured. For instance, Peter would not have asserted that the donkey of the following verse, which marks the quiet beginning of Moses's epic quest to liberate his people, was born to be caught and killed: "So Moses took his wife and his sons, put them on a donkey, and went back to the land of Egypt; and Moses carried the staff of GOD in his hand" (Ex 4:20). Likewise, Peter would not have asserted that all wild animals were born to be caught and killed, among them the ravens GOD refers to in one of His sets of instructions to Elijah:

The word of the LORD came to him, saying, "Go from here and turn eastward, and hide yourself by the Wadi Cherith, which is east of the Jordan. You shall drink from the wadi, and I have commanded the ravens to feed you there." So he went and did according to the word of the LORD; he went and lived by the Wadi Cherith, which is east of the Jordan. The ravens brought him bread and meat in the morning, and bread and meat in the evening; and he drank from the wadi. (1Kings 17:2-6).

Furthermore, Peter would have understood the implications of the following verse, spoken to GOD by Jeremiah:

How long will the land mourn,
and the grass of every field wither?
For the wickedness of those who live in it,
the animals and the birds are swept away,
and because people said, "He is blind to our ways." (Jer 12:4)

Here, wickedness drives away wild animals, with the implication that their presence bodes well for humans. Peter would not have dismissed this interconnection, established by GOD, by asserting that all wild animals were born to be caught and killed. The presence of wild animals is a harbinger of living conditions that favor people too; and Peter, like Jeremiah, would have welcomed their presence.

Finally, Peter presumably was aware, as Paul appeared to be (1Cor 15:32), of the Roman gladiatorial games of his time, which sometimes pitted gladiators against wild animals captured for that purpose. It could be argued that Peter was alluding to those animals when he wrote his second Epistle; but Peter would not have looked to the Roman Empire for an authoritative, spiritual model of any kind. Rome oversaw Christ's crucifixion, and Rome later would arrest Peter himself (Acts 12:3). Surely, then, if in fact that initially misguided empire had deemed its blood-sport captives "born to be caught and killed," Peter still would not have allowed its pagan judgment to influence the inspired thinking that informs his second Epistle.

Wolves in Sheep's Clothing. With the caveat that the Bible gives several accounts of animals' justifiably preying on people, the animals that best fit Peter's description are predatory individuals that make the mistake of hunting humans, animals like the lion that Samson killed (Judg 14:6). From this perspective, Peter's writing can be seen as an elaboration on Christ's likening false prophets to wolves in sheep's clothing (Mt 7:15), a comparison Paul also elaborated on in his speech to the Ephesian elders (Acts 20:29-30). Peter writes that the false prophets are bold, willful, and unafraid to slander angels. Lone animals that prey on humans make good metaphors for false prophets: they are so bold and willful that they do not perceive the danger that people pose to them, just as false prophets do not perceive the might and power of angels. The irrational nature of these lone predators stands out in that it puts them in harm's way; apparently, somehow, the fear of humans that GOD places in animals does not register with them. These individuals were born to be caught and killed. The other members of their species do not make the mistake that they do; although the others hunt, they do not hunt humans. Rational people do not put themselves at the mercy of irrational animals. When animals attempt to prey on them, people kill the animals in self-defense. Similarly, when false prophets attempt to prey on believers, the believers defend their faith.

Another reason that these lone predators fit Peter's description well is that their behavior would elicit Peter's angry tone. Being protective of themselves and their loved ones, people react angrily to predatory threats. If Peter was in fact envisaging animals that prey on humans, then his anger would constitute a typical human reaction to them. In his first Epistle, in a verse mentioned in chapter 2 of *The Value of Animals*, Peter makes a comparison that could have arisen from the same inspiration GOD gave him when he wrote his second Epistle:

Discipline yourselves, keep alert. Like a roaring lion your adversary the devil prowls around, looking for someone to devour. (1Pet 5:8)

Here, Peter portrays the devil as the sort of animal that his second Epistle characterizes as being irrational, instinctual, and born to be caught and killed. Peter might have had the same kind of animal in mind when he wrote about the devil's followers, the false prophets of Second Peter.

Finally, Peter indicates that the animals he writes of will be destroyed, and the false prophets along with them. This lends support to the maneater scenario. As noted in chapter 6, GOD holds animals culpable for certain abominable sins such as sexual relations with women and trespass on sacred ground. Murder makes the list as well. Mosaic law calls for an ox that has gored a person to death to be stoned to death itself (Ex 21:28), a law that derives from GOD's decree that the taking of human life, whether by another human or an animal, should be punished with death (Gen 9:5). If an ox bears responsibility for goring a person, then it stands to reason that a predatory animal would bear responsibility for preying on a person. The dreadful fate that Peter's irrational animals face suggests that they bear responsibility for some wrong they have committed. Predatory animals that unjustifiably murder or attempt to murder would bear such responsibility, and this detail all but completes the picture Peter was painting, an unmistakable picture of individual animals that prey on people.

The Error of the Lawless. Throughout the second chapter of his second Epistle, GOD inspired Peter to compare the false prophets to animals. He compares them to a dog that returns to its vomit (see Prov 26:11), and he compares them to a sow that is washed only to return to its wallowing in the mud. He also compares them to Balaam, who was "rebuked for his own transgressions: a speechless donkey spoke with human voice and restrained the prophet's madness" (see Num 22:28).

The purpose of GOD's inspiration was to illustrate in a memorable and forceful way that false prophets do not live up to the standards He sets, that they fail to harness the powers of logic and moral reasoning that He blesses us with. They scoff at GOD's blessings and act like animals engaged in their lowest forms of behavior.

Like other writers of the Bible, Peter drew on the animal world to make points about the human world with it. The Second Book of Peter sets itself apart by accentuating so strongly one of the few animal behaviors that provoke our righteous anger, predatory behavior toward humans. This approach prepares us to respond strongly to the urgent message Peter concludes with:

You therefore, beloved, since you are forewarned, beware that you are not carried away with the error of the lawless and lose your own stability. But grow in the grace and knowledge of our LORD and Savior Jesus Christ. To him be the glory both now and to the day of eternity. Amen. (2Pet 3:17-18)

We might bridle at the thought that animals' predation on humans serves some higher purpose, but in this case it does. GOD gives no indication that we should suppress our anger toward it; rather, He stirs our passions in order to drive home the message that false prophets go for the throat. So, we may acknowledge the animals' role, however dubious, in developing this message, but, in conclusion, we don't have to like it.

11 ECONOMICS II

Jesus's words and actions uphold the Old Testament's teachings in regard to the economic value of animals. Jesus acknowledges their economic value, but he does not reduce them to it; with his parables and figures of speech, he reaffirms the animals' special place in GOD's Creation. Furthermore, in an exchange with the Pharisee Nicodemus, Jesus shows that he does not overvalue animals by idolizing them. Finally, Jesus's disruption of the Temple features several economic lessons, one of which concerns the animals that were being sold there.

In encouraging them not to fear as they undertook their independent missions, Jesus asked his Disciples to consider the sparrow (Mt 10:29-31). In those times, the sparrow was thought of as an inexpensive, edible bird, and Jesus remarked to the Disciples that two were sold for a penny. As noted in chapter 1, Jesus then reminded them how much more valuable sparrows are than half a penny, saying that not one of them falls to the earth apart from GOD. He went on to remind them that they themselves were worth more than many sparrows and that GOD was mindful of them, too. So, in the space of three sentences, Jesus reiterated three truths: animals have economic value; animals are worth so much more than their economic value that GOD watches over them; and we humans, who occupy a higher place in GOD's spiritual hierarchy, are worth more than animals.

In another sermon, as he foretells his Second Coming, Jesus alludes again to animals' economic value, saying he will separate the sheep from the goats (Mt 25:32). Sheep's wool was more prized than goat's hair [though GOD's blueprint for the Tabernacle called for curtains of goat's hair (Ex 26:7)], and, accordingly, Jesus uses the sheep as a symbol of the saved, and the goats as a symbol of the unsaved. The animals' unequal economic values make for an efficacious metaphor, but the metaphor leaves undisturbed the animals' supra-economic standing with GOD.

Idolatry. In his Epistle to the Romans, the Apostle Paul decries the degeneration of the wicked into the practice of animal idolatry:

Claiming to be wise, they became fools; and they exchanged the glory of the immortal GOD for images resembling a mortal human being or birds or four-footed animals or reptiles. (Rom 1:22-23)

As mentioned in chapter 5, idolators crafted many of their idols in the form of animals. They overvalued animals, ascribing to them godlike powers. Meanwhile, Jesus provides us with a model for making good use of an animal's image, without exchanging the glory of GOD for it.

As he tries to explain his place in GOD's Plan to the confrontational Pharisee Nicodemus, Jesus says, "And just as Moses lifted up the serpent in the wilderness, so must the Son of Man be lifted up, that whoever believes in him may have eternal life" (Jn 3:14-15). Unlike those who descended into the practice of idolizing Moses's serpent (2Kings 18:4), Jesus takes a moral approach to it, invoking it as a symbol for the sole purpose of making his meaning clearer to us (in part, through the haunting similarity his words suggest between the serpent's being raised up by Moses and his being raised up on the cross). Jesus gives the serpent its due, but in comparison to the Son of Man, who grants eternal life, the serpent emerges as the object that it was, limited by GOD in its power and its scope. Jesus took it in hand one last time and, in the process, demonstrated to us how to maintain a moral perspective on the tool vis-a-vis the Toolmaker.

The Temple Disruption. Via the Temple disruption and in its wake, Jesus sends a message about money: let it go. To begin with, he overturned the money changers' tables (Mk 11:15). When he returned to the Temple the next day and was asked, insidiously, whether taxes should be paid to the Roman emperor, he replied, "Give to the emperor the things that are the emperor's, and to GOD the things that are GOD's" (Mk 12:17). Later in the day, he sat outside the Temple treasury and watched as people made contributions to it. There, he witnessed the poor widow whom he lauded for contributing all her money to the treasury (Mk 12:42-44). In purely financial terms, she contributed little, but she won Jesus's praise for letting go and placing herself entirely in GOD's hands.

In contrast stood the Temple merchants, many of whom sold animals to be sacrificed. Jesus accused them of turning the Temple into a den of thieves, as, long before, Jeremiah prophesied they would (Jer 7:11). It is written in the Book of Proverbs that greedy people stir up strife (Prov 28:25), an insight that applies to the Temple merchants and their ignorantly provoking the disruption. In his Epistle to the Colossians, Paul puts greed in the category of idolatry (Col 3:5). From the Proverb's and Paul's wisdom, it follows that the greedy merchants were practicing idolatry in the House of GOD. They were worshipping money, and as a consequence to animals, the merchants were undervaluing them. They were reducing them to their economic value by selling them to be killed in an empty ritual – a ritual that Christ soon would put to an end among his followers.

12 SACRIFICE II

During his lifetime, Jesus repeated the lesson that humans had failed to implement animal sacrifice in the spirit that GOD had intended – that is, as an exercise in humility, mercy, honesty, integrity, and other morals. His and his Disciples' teachings echo the teachings of the Old Testament prophets on humans' corruption of the practice. Nevertheless, the New Testament records some instances of animal sacrifice in its accounts of Christ and the Apostles. Where the details are sparse, we may have faith that these sacrifices were made in the spirit GOD intended and did not render the New Testament's holy people hypocrites. Christ's death and animal sacrifice will be intertwined with each other eternally, with the latter contributing background and vocabulary that help us to grasp the significance of the former.

Jesus and Animal Sacrifice. In his Sermon on the Mount, Jesus tells his listeners that they should defer offering gifts at the altar until they have reconciled any differences with a brother or sister (Mt 5:23-24). Inasmuch as this wisdom restates the moral of the story of Cain and Abel, it illustrates how completely people had missed the point of sacrificial rites. The moral of the very first offering ever made to GOD – Cain's offering, which GOD rejected – was that offerings could not substitute for our making earnest efforts to conduct ourselves morally (Gen 4:6-7). In the following condemnation of some scribes and Pharisees in the Temple, Jesus makes direct reference to Cain's and Abel's story:

"You snakes, you brood of vipers! How can you escape being sentenced to hell? Therefore, I send you prophets, sages, and scribes, some of whom you will kill and crucify, and some you will flog in your synagogues and pursue from town to town, so that upon you may come all the righteous blood shed on earth, from the blood of righteous Abel to the blood of Zechariah son of Barachiah, whom you murdered between the sanctuary and the altar. Truly I tell you, all this will come upon this generation." (Mt 23:33-36).

Much time had passed since Cain had made the first offering, and Jesus's having to raise the specter that he raises here brings to the fore people's chronic deafness to the lessons behind "the blood of righteous Abel."

That is but one instance of several in which Jesus reinforces the Old Testament message that following the spirit of GOD's sacrificial law mattered more than following its letter. In another instance Jesus spoke with a scribe in the Temple, who recognized his mastery of Scripture:

Then the scribe said to him, "You are right, Teacher; you have truly said that 'He is one and besides Him there is no other;' and 'to love Him with all the heart, and with all the understanding, and with all the strength,' and 'to love one's neighbor as oneself' – this is much more important than all whole burnt offerings and sacrifices."
When Jesus saw that he answered wisely, he said to him, "You are not far from the kingdom of GOD." After that, no one dared to ask him any question. (Mk 12:32-34)

The scribe volunteered the comment about "whole burnt offerings and sacrifices;" Jesus did not solicit it. The scribe had come to see that animal sacrifice amounted to mere ritual and did not approach the realm of virtue. It had become a sign of the human race's inability to abide in the Old Covenant and of the need for a New Covenant.

Jesus twice invoked the first half of verse Hosea 6:6, "For I desire steadfast love and not sacrifice." He made the first invocation in response to the Pharisees' questioning his decision to dine with sinners and tax collectors. Jesus said to them, "Go and learn what this means, 'I desire mercy, not sacrifice.' For I have come to call not the righteous, but sinners" (Mt 9:13). Jesus invoked the verse the second time in response to the Pharisees' accusation that the Disciples were breaking the Sabbath by plucking and eating heads of grain on it. Jesus said to the Pharisees, "But if you had known what this means, 'I desire mercy and not sacrifice,' you would not have condemned the guiltless. For the Son of Man is LORD of the Sabbath" (Mt 12:7-8).

In these contexts, the mercy Jesus speaks of is intended for people – for the sinners and taxpayers in the first instance, and for the hungry Disciples in the second. Nevertheless, in this concise statement, his juxtaposition of the word "mercy" and the contrasting word "sacrifice" suggests that the statement may be applied to animals, too. To the degree that the statement calls animals to mind, Jesus would have known that it would. So, at a minimum, he would not count it sinful of us to apply the statement to animals, in addition to humans.

As required by Mosaic law (Ex 13:11-13), a sacrifice was made for the baby Jesus, the firstborn son of Mary (Lk 2:22-24). Also, as required, a lamb was sacrificed for the Last Supper, because it took place on Passover (Deut 16:1-7; Lk 22:7). The Bible gives no further details about these two sacrifices. Jesus sent the Apostles Peter and John to prepare the Passover meal (Lk 22:8), but the Bible does not indicate

33

whether they took part in the rites of sacrifice themselves. We may assume that these sacrifices were made in the right spirit. On the occasions of Jesus's coming into the world and of his departing it, we may trust that GOD would not have allowed His preordained sacrifices to be made without earnest effort. They would not have been perfect sacrifices, but, as a matter of faith, we may be confident that the people involved put forth their best efforts.

Paul and Animal Sacrifice. When, during his ministry, Paul returned to Jerusalem, James and the elders of the nascent church there informed him that many of the city's Jews regarded him as a heretic (Acts 21:20-22). The elders suggested that, in order to appease the Jews, Paul participate with some Nazirites in a purification rite. A sacrifice would follow the purification rite, but only after a seven-day waiting period, in accordance with the law that governed Nazirites (Num 6). Paul participated in the initial rite, but before the appointed time of the sacrifice, a mob of unswayed Jews attacked him. The occupying Romans arrested him (Acts 21:30-33), and eventually he and some of his Jewish accusers were summoned to state their cases before the Roman Governor Felix. Speaking of his return to Jerusalem and of his participation in the Nazirite purification rite, Paul said, "Now after some years I came to bring alms to my nation and to offer sacrifices" (Acts 24:17). It is not unlikely that Paul would have offered the prescribed sacrifice after the waiting period had elapsed. He had participated in the initial rite in order to assuage the Jews. He would have defeated his purpose by choosing not to finish what he had started; the Jews would have interpreted that as a flouting of GOD's law.

Still, the writings of early Christians, like Paul, attest to their rejection of animal sacrifice as a means of atonement. For example, the Epistle to the Hebrews contains the following verses, about Jesus:

For it is fitting that we have such a high priest, holy, blameless, undefiled, separated from sinners, and exalted above the heavens. Unlike the other high priests, he has no need to offer sacrifices day after day, first for his own sins, and then for those of the people; this he did once for all when he offered himself. (Heb 7:26-27)

But, in Jerusalem, Paul, James, and the elders recognized that unless he took some conciliatory measures, Paul would fail to make any inroads with the Jews who distrusted him. In his first Epistle to the Corinthians, Paul addresses this dynamic:

For though I am free with respect to all, I have made myself a slave to all, so that I might win more of them. To the Jews I became as a Jew, in order to win Jews. To those under the law, I became as one under the law (though I myself am not under the law) so that I might win those under the law. (1Cor 9:19-20)

This strategy of Paul's conforms to Jesus's message, stressed in chapter 23 of the Gospel of Matthew, that religious leaders ought to subordinate mechanics to meaning, ritual to righteousness. Paul would have seen the righteousness in endeavoring to win over Jerusalem's Jews by participating in a single rite of Judaic, animal sacrifice. His ambition to guide people toward eternal salvation would have made the sacrifice acceptable both under the Old, if by then obsolete, Covenant and under the New Covenant. As with Jesus's disruption of the Temple, concern for animals did not drive Paul's ambition; but, likewise, the animals would have benefited from it, in that any converts would have ceased making animal sacrifices. So, in this segment of his travels, Paul demonstrated that he took to heart a central theme of Jesus's ministry, the theme that substance is as thunder to the squeaky hinge of style – and the animals could not have suffered for it.

The Temple Disruption. Jesus's disruption of the Temple targeted issues whose importance dwarfed the importance of the animals that the merchants were selling there at the time. Jesus did not treat the animals cruelly, but neither did he coddle them:

The Passover of the Jews was near, and Jesus went up to Jerusalem. In the Temple, he found people selling cattle, sheep, and doves, and the money changers seated at their tables. Making a whip of cords, he drove all of them out of the Temple, both the sheep and the cattle. He also poured out the coins of the money changers and overturned their tables. He told those who were selling the doves, "Take these things out of here! Stop making my Father's House a marketplace!" His Disciples remembered that it was written, "Zeal for Your House will consume me." (Jn 2:13-17)

Consumed by zeal for his Father's House (Ps 69:9), Jesus made the animals a secondary consideration, at best. Nevertheless, as with his invocation of verse Hosea 6:6, Jesus would not deem it sinful of us to view his driving the animals out of the Temple as a show of mercy. On a small scale, Jesus acted as the keeper of those animals; on a large scale, he acts as protector of all the animals his own sacrifice has spared from the futile ritual of animal sacrifice. The keeper on the small scale prefigures the large-scale protector, and the Bible's account of the Temple disruption invites us to appreciate the enduring mercy Jesus has shown the animals.

"I desire mercy, not sacrifice" – it is a lesson that can be applied without difficulty to the animals that might have been sacrificed if the Old Covenant had not been superseded. Still, Jesus does not want us to take a narrow view of it. After he had driven out the merchants and the money changers, the blind and the lame approached him in the Temple and he cured them there (Mt 21:14). On that day, the Temple was dedicated to mercy toward people and animals alike, and not to sacrifice.

The Sacrifice of the Christ. Immediately after Jesus drove out the animals, he was in the presence of the altar as the sole remaining preordained sacrifice. Jesus showed the animals mercy, he showed the blind and the lame mercy, but he himself was destined for sacrifice, not mercy. In its explications of his sacrifice, the New Testament relies on the language of animal sacrifice. The Book of Hebrews contains an example of this:

But when Christ came as a high priest of the good things that have come, then through the greater and perfect tent (not made with hands, that is, not of this creation), he entered once for all into the Holy Place, not with the blood of goats and calves, but with his own blood, thus obtaining eternal redemption. For if the blood of goats and bulls, with the sprinkling of the ashes of a heifer, sanctifies those who have been defiled so that their flesh is purified, how much more will the blood of Christ, who through the eternal Spirit offered himself without blemish to GOD, purify our conscience from dead works to worship the living GOD! (Heb 9:11-14)

In this passage, the tent is analogous to the Tabernacle (Num 9:15); and the Holy Place, or heaven, is analogous to the Tabernacle's inner sanctum. Christ's blood is analogous to animal blood, which, on the annual Day of Atonement, the High Priest would dash on the Mercy Seat, where GOD abided within the inner sanctum (Lev 16:15-19). The eternal redemption that Christ obtained for us overrides, for example, the Old Covenant's aforementioned requirement that a sacrifice be made in order to redeem every firstborn son. Finally, Christ's offering himself "without blemish" harks back to Mosaic laws that stipulated that only animals without blemish would be accepted by GOD as sin offerings (e.g., Lev 6:6).

Christians know this language well. The human race failed in its efforts to carry out sacrificial rites as GOD would have had them carried out. However, in His wisdom, GOD used this failure first to alert us to our shortcomings and then, via the language of animal sacrifice, to frame for us the story of those shortcomings' being forgiven. That story involved the perfect sacrifice, which humans could not achieve.

Ultimately, many animals gave their lives in the service of GOD's authorship of the Bible and the unfurling of His Plan. From the Book of Genesis to the Book of Revelation, stories and images of animal sacrifice are woven into the Bible's fabric. Of the many contexts in which GOD writes of animals, the special case of animal sacrifice might merit a special feeling of gratitude in us. Animal sacrifice helped to set the stage for our salvation. The language of the New Testament reflects that contribution, and so we will be reminded of it forever. All the more reason to treat animals well now.

13 SUFFERING II

The Temple disruption features one of the few direct interactions between Jesus and animals that the Bible records. Another is his interaction with the herd of swine that he permitted some demons to possess, an ostensibly callous act that nonetheless can be reconciled with the Bible's theme of mercy. Occasionally, the Bible alludes to animal husbandry practices that do not ring of mercy; however, Jesus implicitly teaches us not to let those practices distract us from Holy Book's predominant message of mercy.

Jesus and the Swine. The Gospels according to Matthew (Mt 8) and Luke (Lk 8) both recount Jesus's ministry in Gadara. When Jesus arrived there, he was met by a demon-possessed man, mentioned in chapter 8 of *The Value of Animals*. Many demons had entered the man; when Jesus asked, "What is your name?" they answered "Legion," indicating that they were as numerous as the troops in a legion, or division, of the Roman army – approximately five thousand. Fearing him, the demons begged Jesus not to send them back into the abyss and asked instead to be sent into a nearby herd of swine. Jesus obliged, and when the demons entered the swine, the swine rushed into a nearby lake and drowned.

Like many other biblical writings, this story involves animals but does not purport to reveal its own ramifications for them. Jesus doubtless looked as kindly upon swine as he did upon other animals. GOD had declared them unclean and had forbidden the consumption of their meat, but through Jesus, He soon would reverse that guidance. Irrespective of that change, though, Jesus conceivably might have sent the demons into the swine in deference to adherents to the kosher diet, who probably would have countenanced the possession of the swine more readily than of a clean species.

To consider his general assessment of swine from another angle, Jesus harbored no fondness for their more unappealing habits, but he accepted these behaviors without bother. In the Sermon on the Mount, he tells us not to throw our pearls before swine (Mt 7:6); in his parable of the prodigal son, he says that the prodigal son had become so hungry that he would have eaten pig food (Lk 15:16). This imagery is rooted in the domestic swine's being associated with muck and low-grade food, but, following in the biblical tradition, Jesus holds the swine blameless for this. Without questioning swine behavior, Jesus translates for us two observations of that behavior into two memorable lessons.

The story of the possessed swine leaves open the possibility that the swine met a happy fate and the demons an abysmal fate. Jesus would have known the respective fates that awaited them. Perhaps, in ignorance of how the swine would react to being possessed, the demons were asking to be sent down a road that led to the abyss, only indirectly. As to their experience, the swine apparently felt impelled and unafraid to plunge into the lake, an unnatural behavior that calls into question how much, or even if, they suffered as they died. Animals' natural impulse is to avoid suffering, and that the swine rushed to their deaths indicates that, somehow, they might have drowned without suffering.

Meanwhile, although it recalls the High Priest's loading the people's sins onto the archetypal "scapegoat" of Yom Kippur (Lev 16:20-22), this episode also exhibits characteristics of animal sacrifice as GOD had intended it to be. Jesus's driving the demons out of the possessed man succeeded in cleansing him, an immediate outcome on the order of the targeted Temple cleansing sin and guilt offerings were intended to effect. As Jesus was preparing to depart, the man asked him if he could go with him. Jesus counseled him to go home and to spread the Good News, and the man did so. Jesus gained disciples in him and in the untold number this story has inspired through the ages; and that, in turn, is the sort of enduring outcome that GOD had wanted animal sacrifice to bring.

From a final point of view, when Jesus gave the demons permission to enter the swine, he did so with an authoritative, one-word command: "Go!" This no-nonsense dismissal shows that he regarded the demons to be a waste of his time and breath. He dispatched with them quickly and unceremoniously, and he went on to the pressing task of performing several more miracles that day.

So, he despised the demons and not the swine. We may trust that he would have graced the swine with the best eternity an animal can have. Also, in a recurring theme, he knew that he soon would eliminate the need for animal sacrifice and that the more converts his new disciple won, the fewer the sacrifices that might be made. Throughout it, the special knowledge Jesus possessed would have allowed him to manage this sacrifice-like incident with humanity.

Husbandry. The Bible mentions many of the implements used by shepherds and others who worked with animals. They used whips and bridles (Prov 26:3). They used goads, or prods (Ecc 12:11). At times, they enclosed calves in stalls, though, as indicated in the following passage from the Book of Malachi, they later would let them out and so relieve them of their boredom and discomfort:

See, the day is coming, burning like an oven, when all the arrogant and all evildoers will be stubble; the day that comes shall burn them up, says the LORD of hosts, so that it will leave them neither root nor branch. But for you who revere my name, the sun of righteousness shall rise, with healing in its wings. You shall go out leaping like calves from the stall. And you shall tread down the wicked, for they will be ashes under the soles of your feet, on the day when I act, says the LORD of hosts. (Mal 4:1-3)

Whether aids such as the stall were used in a moral way depended on the user, and the story of Balaam and his donkey, for example, communicates a divine expectation of moral use: recall that the angel upbraided Balaam for striking his donkey (Num 22:32).

A practice of the time that caused animals pain was the practice of branding, a suitable metaphor for the self-defeating behavior of the faithless, as in the following verse from the Book of Isaiah:

But all of you are kindlers of fire,
lighters of firebrands.
Walk in the flame of your fire,
and among the brands that you have kindled!
This is what you shall have from my hand:
you shall lie down in torment. (Isa 50:11)

Among the Israelites, the use of firebrands might be explained by the existence of laws that could be enforced only if an animal's owner could be identified – for example, laws that required stray animals be returned to their owners (Deut 22:1-3) or that owners be compensated justly for the theft of their animals (Ex 22:1-4). The owners themselves, who gave their animals names (e.g., Isa 43:1-2; Jn 10:3), probably could identify them without relying on a brand, but others might have relied on the brand in their search for an animal's owner.

Finally, in the case of the sheep, for instance, the economic value of the animal lay in its being sheared periodically and, eventually, slaughtered. In these regards, the animal's limited intelligence and lack of perspective can be a blessing from GOD. We customarily view "the silence of the lambs" designated for slaughter as a dark, foreboding image, and the Bible takes the same view, which is shaped by humans' foreknowledge of the lambs' imminent fate. But a lamb's silence may indicate that it has not been treated inhumanely in the days and hours leading up to its slaughter, that it has not been worked into a state of agitation or deprivation by ill-treatment during the lead-up. When the Bible depicts a sheep as going silently to its shearer (Isa 53:7), or a lamb or an ox (Prov 7:22) as going silently to slaughter, it incidentally might be giving us a glimpse of a husbandry system that was founded on humanity. Animals' cognitive limitations can be a blessing if we let them be. We can spare animals a dreadful death by treating them well to the very end.

When Jesus identifies himself as the Good Shepherd, he invites considerations like these. The Good Shepherd shows mercy; the Good Shepherd protects; the Good Shepherd gives of himself to his sheep and does not abandon them to danger. Jesus's adopting this persona for himself adds a crowning touch to the Bible's collection of allegories, parables, analogies, metaphors, and similes that allude to shepherds and shepherding. The Good Shepherd is a figure undergirded with the steelwork of GOD's Word, as befits the Person of the Messiah.

14 THE GOOD SHEPHERD

Although the Bible often treats sheep and shepherds as symbols, in doing so it also gives us an accurate impression of their daily lives. A look at some of its less celebrated – though perfect – comparisons supports this. Its more celebrated comparisons depict a relationship between shepherds and their sheep that features caring, consideration, and mercy. The "Good" in "Good Shepherd" has moral connotations, as shown not only through the lower-case good shepherds of the Bible but also, by negative example, through the bad. Jesus's own characterization of the Good Shepherd illustrates the great lengths to which shepherds would go in the service of their sheep. Jesus honors the literal good shepherd by identifying himself as the figurative Good Shepherd. Good shepherds behave in righteous ways. Their caring relationship with their sheep has been written into the Bible for eternity, as an analogy for Jesus's relationship with us. Through the ages, people have found comfort in this analogy; it is timeless and universal.

The Shepherding Life. By reading the Bible, we learn, for example, that the shepherd's life was nomadic; that would-be shepherds had to prove their worth before they would be entrusted with the responsibilities of shepherding; that shepherding could be dirty work; and that predators took their toll on sheep and shepherds. The prophet Isaiah quotes a writing of King Hezekiah in which the king describes his state of mind during a bout of illness he had suffered not long before:

I said, "I shall not see the LORD
in the land of the living;
I shall look upon mortals no more
among the inhabitants of the world.
My dwelling is plucked up and removed from me
like a shepherd's tent;
like a weaver I have rolled up my life;
he cuts me off from the loom;
from day to night you bring me to an end. (Isa 38:11-12)

The reference to a shepherd's tent relates to shepherds' practice of dwelling in tents during the extended stops they made to graze, water, or rest their flocks.

Psalm 78 tells of GOD's choosing David to lead Israel:

He chose His servant David,
and took him from the sheepfolds;
from tending the nursing ewes He brought him
to be the shepherd of his people Jacob,
of Israel, his inheritance.
With upright heart he tended them,
and guided them with skillful hand. (Ps 78:70-72)

From this passage we learn that a period of work in the sheepfolds may have preceded a promotion to shepherding.

In the verse below, Job contrasts the predicament he finds himself in with a time when young men were so in awe of him that they would retreat from his presence:

But now they make sport of me,
those who are younger than I,
whose fathers I would have disdained
to set with the dogs of my flock. (Job 30:1)

This verse alludes to the sheepdogs that assisted the shepherds with their work.

In the following verse, GOD speaks of King Nebuchadnezzar of Babylon, whom He was sending to conquer Egypt:

He shall kindle a fire in the temples of the gods of Egypt; and he shall burn them and carry them away captive; and he shall pick clean the land of Egypt, as a shepherd picks his cloak clean of vermin; and he shall depart from there safely. (Jer 43:12)

This verse dispels any notion that shepherding was a glamorous occupation.

Finally, the Bible gives us a concrete sense of the menace that predatory animals were to shepherds. For example, In the Book of Isaiah, GOD portrays himself as a lion that is undaunted by the shouts of shepherds who have banded together to scare it off (Isa 31:4). And the Book of Amos contains the following grisly verse, which alludes to surrogate shepherds' practice of gathering evidence of a predatory attack, with which they could demonstrate to an animal's owner that it was lost to predation and not to theft or incompetence:

Thus says the LORD: *As a shepherd rescues from the mouth of the lion two legs or a piece of an ear, so shall the people of Israel who live in Samaria be rescued, with the corner of a couch and part of a bed. (Am 3:12)*

So, the Bible presents an authentic version of the shepherd's existence, and not some sanitized or idealized version. And the authentic version features a human commitment to animals so strong that it turns the world on its head.

Good Shepherding. In a prophecy that GOD would break a siege of Jerusalem, Isaiah imagines Him as a shepherd:

He will feed His flock like a shepherd;
He will gather the lambs in His arms,
and carry them in his bosom,
and gently lead the mother sheep. (Isa 40:11)

This image gives us a sense of the shepherd's intimate, personal connection to his sheep. The shepherd protects the lambs by carrying them "in his bosom," and, at the same time, he attends to the needs of the mother sheep, which, themselves, would feel protective of the lambs. The shepherd might even recall a time when he carried those mother sheep in his bosom, when they were lambs. These sorts of interactions with sheep would foster in shepherds feelings of closeness to and affection for the sheep, as attested by the tender language of verses like Isaiah's.

The Book of Genesis relates the story of Jacob's encounter with Esau, his brother, after a long separation. Jacob had stolen Esau's birthright (Gen 25:31), and out of fear of reprisal, he wanted to avoid traveling with Esau and the horde of four hundred men that accompanied him. When Esau proposed that they travel together, Jacob gave this response:

But Jacob said to him, "My lord knows that the children are frail and that the flocks and herds, which are nursing, are a care to me; and if they are overdriven for one day, all the flocks will die. Let my lord pass on ahead of his servant, and I will lead on slowly, according to the pace of the cattle that are before me and according to the pace of the children, until I come to my lord in Seir." (Gen 33:13-14)

Although Jacob spoke these words in order to rid himself of Esau, they tell of a herder's sensitivity to his animals' needs. Jacob will let the animals and the children set the pace. He will accommodate the mother animals' pausing to nurse their young. He will not overdrive them.

By implication, the Bible's portrayals of cruel shepherding speak to the care involved in good shepherding. In the following passage, which concerns the Babylonian Exile, GOD gives the prophet Ezekiel a damning message for Israel's leaders:

The word of the LORD *came to me: Mortal, prophesy against the shepherds of Israel; prophesy and say to them – to the shepherds: Thus says the* LORD GOD: *Ah, you shepherds of Israel who have been feeding yourselves! Should not shepherds feed the sheep? You eat the fat, you clothe yourselves with the wool, you slaughter the fatlings; but you do not feed the sheep. You have not strengthened the weak, you have not healed the sick, you have not bound up the injured, you have not brought back the strayed, you have not sought the lost, but with force and harshness you have ruled them. So they were scattered, because there was no shepherd; and scattered, they became food for all the wild animals. My sheep were scattered, they wandered over all the mountains and on every high hill; my sheep were scattered over all the face of the earth, with no one to search or seek for them. (Ezek 34:1-6)*

These verses imply that GOD measures the goodness of good shepherding in terms of nurturance, commitment, and mercy. Shepherds have moral obligations to their sheep; good shepherds fulfill those obligations.

The Good Shepherd. Jesus's description of the Good Shepherd captures the essence of his mission here on earth. Speaking in Jerusalem, Jesus emphasizes the Good Shepherd's willingness to lay down his life for the sheep. No doubt, this emphasis had its origins in stories of literal good shepherds who were killed in defense of their sheep:

"I am the Good Shepherd. The Good Shepherd lays down his life for the sheep. The hired hand, who is not the Shepherd and does not own the sheep, sees the wolf coming and leaves the sheep and runs away — and the wolf snatches them and scatters them. The hired hand runs away because a hired hand does not care for the sheep. I am the Good Shepherd. I know my own and my own know me, just as the Father knows me and I know the Father. And I lay down my life for the sheep. I have other sheep that do not belong to this fold. I must bring them also, and they will listen to my voice. So there will be one flock, one Shepherd. For this reason the Father loves me, because I lay down my life in order to take it up again. No one takes it from me, but I lay it down of my own accord. I have power to lay it down, and I have power to take it up again. I have received this command from my Father." (Jn 10:11-18)

Unlike the hired hand of this analogy, the Good Shepherd stays with his sheep when he sees the wolf coming, and surely stories circulated among the Jews of good shepherds who fell victim to the wolf.

Jesus discovered in the Good Shepherd a figure that helped him explain to us his role as the Messiah. This attests to the commitment good shepherds brought to the care of their sheep. Even though that commitment was imperfect, Jesus saw in it enough merit to make the Good Shepherd a personification of his devotion to us.

All Places and All Times. Throughout the New Testament and in the Old Testament, Jesus is depicted as the Good Shepherd. In his prophecy of Jesus's incarnation, Micah compares Jesus to a shepherd (Mic 5:2-4). In his first Epistle, the Apostle Peter refers to him as "the Shepherd and Guardian of your souls" (1Pet 2:25). In the Book of Hebrews, he is referred to as "the Great Shepherd" (Heb 13:20).

Jesus also makes further references to himself as a shepherd. Touchingly, as they journeyed to Jerusalem, he said to his Disciples, "Do not be afraid, little flock, for it is your Father's good pleasure to give you the kingdom" (Lk 12:32). In the Gospel of John, during his final appearance to the Disciples, Jesus effectively promoted Peter to the position of shepherd:

When they had finished breakfast, Jesus said to Simon Peter, "Simon son of John, do you love me more than these?"
He said to him, "Yes, LORD, you know that I love you."
Jesus said to him, "Feed my lambs."
A second time he said to him, "Simon son of John, do you love me?"
He said to him, "Yes, LORD, you know that I love you."
Jesus said to him, "Tend my sheep."
He said to him the third time, "Simon son of John, do you love me?"
Peter felt hurt because he said to him the third time, "Do you love me?" And he said to him, "LORD, you know everything. You know that I love you."
Jesus said to him, "Feed my sheep." (Jn 21:15-17)

In this passage, Jesus prompts Peter to recant, indirectly, his three denials of him (Jn 18:15-27), by means of three declarations of love for him. We understand Jesus's instructions to signify that Peter was to nurture the early church and early Christians; Jesus conveys this message with shepherding imagery.

Both Isaiah and Peter declared that the Word of GOD will stand forever (Isa 40:8; 1Pet 1:25). Jesus said that his words never will pass away (Mt 24:35), nor even a single stroke of a single letter of GOD's law, until it has been fulfilled (Mt 5:18). Jesus intended his message to be accessible to and to resonate with people of all places and all times. During his ministry, by making the Good Shepherd as central a figure as he did, he signaled that the figure would in fact remain accessible and resonant. We continue to interpret the Good Shepherd as the embodiment of a personal, concerned, and comforting Savior. We continue to appreciate the godliness of a good shepherd's relationship with his sheep, and this continues to inform our relationship with Jesus.

The Good Shepherd willingly lays down his life for his sheep. The Good Shepherd holds dominion over his sheep. Jesus underscores the virtue of the literal good shepherd's handling of dominion when he compares it favorably to his own handling of dominion over us. Humbleness, selflessness, patience, and love are hallmarks of the godly exercise of dominion. In the writings of the New Testament, animals help to highlight the first of these qualities, humbleness, in Jesus; and they also will carry us directly into a prophecy of his coming, divine dominion.

15 DOMINION II

With its examples of the good and the bad, the New Testament stays true to the Old Testament's lesson that the tenor of a given instance of dominion is determined by the holder of dominion. Christ's ultimate dominion will be absolute, all-encompassing, loving, and blissful. The prophecy of the Triumphal Entry offered by Zechariah weaves together the humbleness of that dominion, of Christ himself, and of an animal. GOD uses the animals of the Bible to give us insight into the nature of Christ, and insight into his nature opens up invaluable opportunities for us to emulate him.

The Tenor of Christ's Dominion. Paul's Epistle to the Romans contains the following verses, which contrast the effects of Adam's original sin with the effects of Christ's sinlessness:

If, because of one man's trespass, death exercised dominion through that one, much more surely will those who receive the abundance of grace and the free gift of righteousness exercise dominion in life through the one man, Jesus Christ.
Therefore, just as one man's trespass led to condemnation for all, so one man's act of righteousness leads to justification and life for all. For just as by the one man's disobedience the many were made sinners, so by the one man's obedience the many will be made righteous. But law came in, with the result that the trespass multiplied; but where sin increased, grace abounded all the more, so that, just as sin exercised dominion in death, so grace might also exercise dominion through justification leading to eternal life through Jesus Christ our LORD. (Rom 5:17-21)

Jesus took dominion from sin and death and gave it to grace and life. Dominion was both taken and given, and the before-and-after contrast illustrates again that the mood of an instance of dominion reflects the spirit of the holder of dominion.

Near the end of his first Epistle to Timothy, Paul offers a prayer that Christ's dominion be eternal (1Tim 6:16). The dominion Paul prays for eclipses all other dominion. In his Epistle to the Colossians, Paul writes that all thrones, dominions, rulers, and powers were created through and for Christ (Col 1:16). He writes to the Ephesians that GOD has seated Christ far above all rule, authority, power, and dominion (Eph 1:20-22). And, in the first Epistle to Timothy, Paul describes Christ as the "only Sovereign," and as the King of kings and the LORD of lords (1Tim 6:15). As revealed in the following passage, the coming dominion promises paradise:

And I saw the holy city, the new Jerusalem, coming down out of heaven from GOD, prepared as a bride adorned for her husband. And I heard a loud voice from the throne saying,
"See, the home of GOD is among mortals.
He will dwell with them;
they will be His peoples,
and GOD Himself will be with them;
He will wipe every tear from their eyes.
Death will be no more;
mourning and crying and pain will be no more,
for the first things have passed away."
And the one who was seated on the throne said, "See, I am making all things new." Also He said, "Write this, for these words are trustworthy and true." Then He said to me, "It is done! I am the Alpha and the Omega, the beginning and the end. To the thirsty I will give water as a gift from the spring of the water of life." (Rev 21:2-6)

Christ made this possible by sacrificing himself to us, an act of perfect love, grace, mercy, selflessness, and humility.

The Triumphal Entry. In one instance, the Bible evokes Christ's humility by way of an animal that figures in his Triumphal Entry into Jerusalem, and in Zechariah's prophecy of that event:

Rejoice greatly, O daughter Zion!
Shout aloud, O daughter Jerusalem!
Lo, your King comes to you;
triumphant and victorious is he,
humble and riding on a donkey,
on a colt, the foal of a donkey.
He will cut off the chariot from Ephraim
and the war horse from Jerusalem;
and the battle bow shall be cut off,
and he shall command peace to the nations;

his dominion shall be from sea to sea,
and from the River to the ends of the earth. (Zech 9:9-10)

In these stirring verses, the donkey attests to Christ's humility. One would expect a triumphant king to appear on, say, a great white stallion, but Christ arrived on the less majestic donkey. The donkey completes the image, which exudes humility, and Zechariah describes a dominion of which that humility will be a hallmark, Christ's coming dominion of peace, unpolluted by the instruments of war.

In connection with the donkey, Christ made a further show of humility when he sent two of his Disciples ahead of him to fetch it. Reminiscent of Samuel's reassuring Saul, on the occasion of his enthronement, that the donkeys he was seeking had been found (1Sam 9:18-20), Christ said to the two Disciples, "If anyone says to you, 'Why are you doing this?' just say this, 'The LORD needs it and will send it back here immediately'" (Mk 11:3-6). In other words, the humble King took the time to address concerns that might be expressed for the donkey. As it turned out, some bystanders did question the Disciples' actions, and the Disciples reassured them with Christ's words. This account gives a nod of approval to the bystanders' concerns, and it gives us a taste of the abundant consideration Christ will show the subjects of his everlasting dominion.

Whether as the Good Shepherd, the Son of Man, or the Lamb of GOD, Jesus places himself beneath us, laying down his life for us (Jn 10:11-18), living among us without a place to lay his head (Mt 8:20), or redeeming us to GOD in lieu of any further animal sacrifice (Heb 7:26-27). Again, in each of these instances, animals serve as vehicles for the expression of his humility. GOD and Jesus have deemed dominion to be an opportunity to serve (Lk 22:24-27). GOD gave us detailed instructions for redeeming ourselves to Him via animal sacrifice, and when we failed to carry out those instructions in the spirit He intended, He took up our cause Himself and sent His only begotten Son to be sacrificed (Jn 3:16) for us, a personal sacrifice on His own part of unfathomable depth. For his part, in an act of perfect submission to and obedience to his Father's will, Jesus voluntarily delivered himself into the hands of his crucifiers (Mt 16:21-23). These actions GOD and Jesus took for our benefit – that is, for the benefit of those over whom they hold dominion. The Father and His Son require nothing of us that would even register on the scale of the hardships they have endured; but they compel us to ask if there are elements of their approach that we can apply to our relationship with those over whom we hold dominion, our animals.

PART III

OUR ANIMALS

16 HUNTING & FISHING

The Bible contains many references to hunting and fishing, and these references offer a glimpse of the methods used during biblical times. The story of Esau, who was a hunter, surfaces several times in the Bible, and it does not reflect well on the hunter's mentality Esau held to. The Bible looks more favorably upon fishing, with Jesus himself producing a miraculous catch of fish; nonetheless, Christians have reason to seek GOD's guidance concerning modern-day fishing practices.

The Book of Job mentions several means of hunting: e.g., nets, pitfalls, snares, and ropes (Job 18:8-10). The pair of Psalms 140 and 141 allude to hunting in several of their stanzas. The Bible devotes five of its verses to the hunter Nimrod, a great grandson of Noah (Gen 10:8-12). Nimrod was king of the land of Shina and of a portion of Assyria, and the Bible describes him as a "mighty warrior" and as a "mighty hunter before the LORD."

Esau's Legacy. As to Esau, who was mentioned in chapter 14 of *The Value of Animals*, one day as his twin brother, Jacob, the younger of the two by a body length, was cooking a lentil stew, Esau returned from the field famished. Esau asked for some of the stew, but before he would give him any of it, Jacob demanded that Esau surrender to him his birthright as the firstborn son (Gen 25:31). Feeling as if he would have died without the food, Esau complied, and his compliance changed the course of history. Jacob's descendants formed the nation of Israel; Esau's, the nation of Edom. While the Bible stipulates that the Edomites were not to be abhorred (Deut 23:7), they did not enjoy GOD's favor as the Israelites did. Isaiah prophesies against Edom (Isa 34); in the Book of Ezekiel, GOD threatens to cut off humans and animals from Edom (Ezek 25:13); and the Book of Obadiah is devoted to a condemnation of Edom.

Esau's choice of lifestyle belies a spiritual starvation that manifested itself in his selling his birthright. The Bible contrasts Esau's lifestyle with the lifestyle of Jacob, whom it characterizes as a simple man, "dwelling in tents" (Gen 25:27). Esau married Mahalath (Gen 28:9), daughter of Ishmael, whom the Bible describes as a "wild ass of a man" (Gen 16:12). The birthright Esau forsook was not an arbitrary privilege; rather, GOD eventually would enshrine it in His law (Deut 21:17). In the Book of Jeremiah (Jer 49:8), GOD threatens Edom with "the calamity of Esau," saying,

> *"But as for me, I have stripped Esau bare,*
> *I have uncovered his hiding places,*
> *and he is not able to conceal himself.*
> *His offspring are destroyed, his kinsfolk,*
> *and his neighbors; and he is no more." (Jer 49:10).*

The Book of Hebrews portrays Esau as being sinful and faithless (Heb 12:16). In the Book of Malachi, GOD says that He has loved Jacob but hated Esau (Mal 1:2-3), a statement Paul alludes to in his Epistle to the Romans (Rom 9:13). On the whole, Esau's tale cautions us not to let an attraction to the hunt draw us into sin.

A Hunting Debate. Some of the northern contiguous states of the United States permit annual deer-hunting seasons, which have prompted debates concerning, for example, how to manage the size of the states' deer herds. The deer hunting season traumatizes deer. Anecdotes are numerous of panic-stricken deer crashing into or through storefront windows during the hunting season, or of shell-shocked deer wandering about in populated areas they normally would not venture into. Deer seek out the relative safety of roadways during the hunting season, and this increases the incidence of automobile collisions with deer. That increase, in turn, is inflated by the authorities' scheduling deer-hunting seasons to take place during the deer's mating season, in autumn, when deer pursue each other and are prone to engage in risky behaviors. The deer's habitat comes under fire, and when the shooting commences, the fear and dread the deer feel must surely be more severe than their normal, inborn fear and dread of us.

Proponents of deer hunting argue that the hunt keeps deer populations in check and therefore spares deer of starvation and the other ill effects of overpopulation. Opponents argue that feeding programs, sponsored by governments at multiple levels and by businesses near popular hunting areas, maintain deer populations at artificially high levels. In the wintertime, deer come out of the woods and line country roads when they hear the feed trucks approach. One potential solution that has been put forth is to conduct a final hunt that would reduce deer herds to sizes just large enough to allow them to sustain themselves over the long term. This is the sort of substantive dialogue that might await Christians engaged via Esau's tale or by other biblical writings cited in *The Value of Animals*.

Fishing. The Apostles Peter and Andrew were fishermen, whom Jesus called to "fish for people" (Mt 4:18-20). Jesus once produced a miraculous catch of fish (Jn 21:6), and so fishing in his mode was a moral activity. When the resurrected Jesus asked the Apostles for something to eat, they served him broiled fish (Lk 24:42-43).

With one exception, the Bible depicts Jesus and the Apostles fishing with nets when they fished. While, in the Book of Ecclesiastes, Solomon labels fishing nets "cruel" (Ecc 9:12), the sense in which he means they are cruel is that they bring fish to a sudden and unexpected end. The broader message Solomon conveys in the surrounding passage is that calamity can befall anyone at any time.

Contemporary commercial practices have little in common with the sort of small-scale net fishing that Jesus and the Apostles engaged in. Jesus's miraculous catch totaled one hundred fifty-three fish, and the Bible's account of it includes the comment, "though there were so many, the net was not torn" (Jn 21:11). A catch of one hundred fifty-three lake fish or sea fish would not strain a modern, high-volume trawl or net. In some areas, commercial fishing has depleted the populations of fish or other aquatic animals, and this does not accord with GOD's will that sea life fill the seas (Gen 1:22). Meanwhile, intensive fish farming has become a large industry the products of which are common on grocers' shelves. By modern standards, when Jesus and the Apostles fished, they fished on a humble scale.

The Gospel of Matthew relates that Jesus once directed Peter to hook a certain fish and, miraculously, to retrieve from its mouth a coin for their Temple tax payment (Mt 17:27). Jesus told Peter that, as children of GOD, they may have withheld the payment but that they would make it anyway, lest they offend the tax collectors. The positive ramifications of this endeavor of Jesus's extend far, and its call for a hook notwithstanding, the faithful still may follow an inspiration of the Spirit to counsel against fishing with hooks in unexceptional circumstances.

The Fish Symbol. The fish joins the lamb and the dove as a familiar Christian symbol. Just as the lamb symbolizes Christ the Redeemer and the dove his Spirit of peace, the fish has come to symbolize the Christ of faith and ministry. On one occasion, Jesus fed five thousand with five loaves of bread and two fish (Mk 6:34-44); on another, he fed four thousand with seven loaves of bread and a few small fish (Mk 8:1-9). These miracles and his miraculous catch of fish exemplify the faith he espoused in his teaching that we ought not to worry about what we will eat (Mt 6:25-27). The fish symbol may continue to remind us of this even if our present-day concerns for animals lead us to make some changes to our diets.

17 DIET

GOD has given us the animals as food (Gen 9:3), but He does not want us to regard them only as food. The Bible makes this known in several places – for example, in its record of the kosher dietary prohibitions against eating the meat of certain animals. Adherence to the kosher diet constituted part of the Jewish identity, but, in the end, the Bible tells a tale of people's having twisted it from being a way to honor GOD into being a basis for judging others. Nevertheless, to his Jewish followers, Jesus's declaring all foods clean represented a sea change. The New Testament Epistles contain several references to diet, and these can be understood against the backdrop of Jesus's declaration. They also give us an opportunity to witness the Holy Spirit at work in the early Christians; and, consequently, they give us an inspiration to allow the Holy Spirit to work in us as we weigh our own dietary options. Animals helped Jesus to communicate to us the distinction between the letter of the law and the spirit of the law, and a reminder of that distinction may bring Christians to change their lifestyles.

Against Excess. With regard to meat consumption, GOD looks dimly upon excesses and other kinds of immoral behavior. For example, during the exodus from Egypt, the people complained about the manna GOD was providing them with, as food, and they bemoaned their lack of meat (Num 11:4-6). When Moses prayed to GOD for meat, GOD gave him these instructions:

"And say to the people: Consecrate yourselves for tomorrow, and you shall eat meat; for you have wailed in the hearing of the LORD, saying, 'If only we had meat to eat! Surely it was better for us in Egypt.' Therefore, the LORD will give you meat, and you shall eat. You shall eat not only one day, or two days, or five days, or ten days, or twenty days, but for a whole month – until it comes out of your nostrils and becomes loathsome to you – because you have rejected the LORD, who is among you, and have wailed before Him, saying, 'Why did we ever leave Egypt?'" (Num 11:18-20)

GOD provided the meat, in the form of quails; but as the people feasted on them, GOD became disgusted with them again. He afflicted them with a plague "while the meat was still between their teeth" (Num 11:33-34).

In the following passage, GOD again cautions against excess:

Do not be among winebibbers,
or among gluttonous eaters of meat;
for the drunkard and the glutton will come to poverty,
and drowsiness will clothe them with rags. (Prov 23:20-21)

In another Proverb, GOD teaches that a dinner of vegetables served in a loving environment is better than marbled beef served in a hateful environment (Prov 15:17).

GOD's kosher dietary rules place many restrictions on meat consumption. Among other purity laws, GOD lays out the dietary rules in chapter 11 of the Book of Leviticus and also in chapter 14 of the Book of Deuteronomy. He uses strong language to describe animals that He forbade the Israelites to eat, calling the animals "unclean" or "detestable" or "abominations." In the Book of Isaiah, GOD speaks out against people who eat the forbidden "flesh of pigs" (Isa 66:17). So, here again, although GOD has given people the animals as food, He forbids sinful indulgence.

The Kosher Diet. In the Book of Leviticus, GOD gives the following explanation as to why He established His kosher dietary rules:

But I have said to you: You shall inherit their land, and I will give it to you to possess, a land flowing with milk and honey. I am the LORD your GOD; I have separated you from the peoples. You shall therefore make a distinction between the clean animal and the unclean, and between the unclean bird and the clean; you shall not bring abomination on yourselves by animal or by bird or by anything with which the ground teems, which I have set apart for you to hold unclean. You shall be holy to me; for I the LORD am holy, and I have separated you from the other peoples to be mine. (Lev 20:24-26)

Thus, GOD's declaring some animals clean and others unclean parallels His separating the Israelites from the other peoples of the world. Mealtime would give the Israelites a chance to honor GOD by obeying His commands. The Israelites embraced the kosher diet. When the theretofore kosher Apostle Peter had a vision of unclean animals and was told to "kill and eat" them (Acts 10:13), he felt called to minister to the Gentiles, who did not subscribe to the kosher diet and ate unclean animals (Acts 11:12). Jews were indoctrinated into the kosher diet as children, and, as Peter's tale suggests, they equated not being kosher with not being Jewish.

The Bible hints that that equation engendered a certain haughtiness in the Jews, and just as they had corrupted sacrificial rites by making them a crutch, they seem to have misconstrued their dietary regulations and made a bludgeon of them. Jesus declared all foods clean after some scribes and Pharisees insinuated that the Disciples had defiled themselves by eating without first washing their hands in the tradition of the Jewish elders (Mk 7:1-23). Jesus said people are not defiled by what goes in but by what comes out of the heart. He said that among the evils that may come out are pride and slander.

These two evils seem to have been at work in adherents to the kosher diet. In his Epistle to them, Paul advises the Colossians not to allow anyone to condemn them in matters of food (Col 2:16). In his Epistle to the Romans, Paul advises the Romans not to pass judgment on each other's dietary choices (Rom 14:3). The sweep of Jesus's declaration that all foods are clean implies that people were being judged unfairly for dietary practices that not only included hand-washing traditions but extended far beyond them as well. Paul's choice of subject matter in his Epistles supports that conclusion; Jesus was targeting the misuse of kosher dietary laws as an instrument of condemnation.

Idols and Spirit. Despite Jesus's teaching, some of the early converts from Judaism struggled with the prospect of abandoning the kosher diet. When Paul advised the Romans not to judge, he addressed his advice to two subgroups: "those who eat" and "those who abstain." By the latter, he meant those who abstained from eating foods that, under the Old Covenant, were unclean. He was addressing a similar subgroup within the Corinthian church when he wrote that they should eat, without compunction, whatever is sold in the meat market (1Cor 10:25). Finally, in his first Epistle to Timothy, Paul writes that no kind of meat should be refused as long as it is accepted with thanksgiving (1Tim 4:4).

Jesus left it to his followers to deal with the question of eating the meat of animals sacrificed to idols. On the surface, if nothing that goes in defiles, then Christians do not defile themselves by eating that meat. This argument notwithstanding, the early church leaders came down on the side of abstaining from eating it. In a word, the early Christians realized that they could make a statement with what they ate; and this realization is addressed by the second half of Jesus's teaching about the cleanliness of foods, the part that says that what comes out can defile a person. Paul captures this dynamic in the first Epistle to the Corinthians:

Consider the people of Israel; are not those who eat the sacrifices partners in the altar? What do I imply then? That food sacrificed to idols is anything, or that an idol is anything? No, I imply that what pagans sacrifice they sacrifice to demons and not to GOD. I do not want you to be partners with demons. You cannot drink the cup of the LORD and the cup of demons. You cannot partake of the table of the LORD and the table of demons. Or are we provoking the LORD to jealousy? Are we stronger than He? (1Cor 10:18-22)

Paul goes on to write that the mere act of eating the meat of animals sacrificed to idols does not defile. He writes that Christians should abstain out of consideration for others, who might misinterpret the act (1Cor 10:28-29). Similarly, in the Epistle to the Romans, Paul cautions Christians not to let what they eat be a stumbling block to others (Rom 14:15-21).

The New Testament's passages concerning dietary restrictions bear witness to the Holy Spirit. A few of the early Christians had it firsthand from Jesus that no food or drink defiles; but as the early Christians pondered the implications of this truth, the Holy Spirit stepped in to prevent them from taking a headlong approach to applying it. Jesus taught us to heed the guidance of the Holy Spirit, as shown in chapter 8 and as Paul explains to the Corinthians, below:

Such is the confidence we have through Christ toward GOD. Not that we are competent of ourselves to claim anything as coming from us; our competence is from GOD, who has made us competent to be ministers of a New Covenant, not of letter but of Spirit; for the letter kills, but the Spirit gives life. (2Cor 3:4-6)

By giving the Holy Spirit the final say on his teachings, Jesus paved the way for Christians of every era to follow the spirit of those teachings without becoming bogged down in their letter.

Past, Present, & Future. In his first Epistle to Timothy, Paul writes that in the end times, people will be deceived by demons that demand abstinence from certain foods (1Tim 4:1-3). The Book of Hebrews cautions against being influenced by "strange teachings" regarding food regulations (Heb 13:9). Among Christians who already have adopted plant-based diets are those who have become wary because they know that when Jesus pronounced all foods clean, he did not give us license to mistreat the animals whose products we eat, just as he did not give us license to partake of pagan sacrifices. These Christians take it into consideration that animals that are raised solely to be slaughtered are feeling and perceiving beings, GOD's creations, before they become food, and that at any given time, the animals that are being used to produce foods such as milk and eggs number in the hundreds of millions. Such consciousness is founded not on strange or demonic teachings but on godly teachings. GOD would be dismayed if we failed at least to factor any mistreatment of animals into our purchasing decisions: after all, if we purchase the products of mistreated animals, then, in effect, we are paying others for having allowed mistreatment to enter into their farming or killing practices.

Until GOD made the Bow Covenant with Noah, humans lived only on vegan foods (Gen 9:3). Daniel thrived on a diet of vegetables while the health of his adversaries, who at the same time were eating foods from pagan sacrifices, declined (Dan 1:8-17). Paul wrote that he would abstain from eating meat if his eating it would cause another to fall (1Cor 8:13). However, he also wrote that weak people eat only vegetables (Rom 14:2). In a milieu where the good shepherd was so highly esteemed that he could represent the Son of GOD in biblical texts (Jn 10:11-18), the latter statement would ring true. Abstinence from eating the products of animals that have been treated scrupulously humanely from birth to death might belie an uninspired departure from GOD's decision to give us the animals as food.

Spirit v. Letter. Life is more than food. Jesus assures us of this as he encourages us to have faith that GOD will provide (Mt 6:25-27). Paul teaches us that the kingdom of GOD is manifested not in food or drink but in "righteousness and peace and joy in the Holy Spirit" (Rom 14:17). He teaches us that food does not commend us to GOD (1Cor 8:8). In other words, nothing abides in food that defiles or sanctifies in and of itself. However, our dietary choices, as distinct from food per se, have a moral dimension to them. In the following passage, Paul cautions us against eating foods that we feel ill at ease about:

But those who have doubts are condemned if they eat, because they do not act from faith; for whatever does not proceed from faith is sin. (Rom 14:23)

In his Epistle to the Philippians, Paul cautions against deifying the "belly:"

For many live as enemies of the cross of Christ; I have often told you of them, and now I tell you even with tears. Their end is destruction; their god is the belly; and their glory is in their shame; their minds are set on earthly things. (Phil 3:18-19)

Finally, Paul writes to the Corinthians, "So, whether you eat or drink, or whatever you do, do everything for the glory of GOD" (1Cor 10:31). This lesson recalls a lesson of the Old Testament:

In all your ways acknowledge Him,
and He will make straight your paths. (Prov 3:6)

Jesus came to fulfill and not to abolish the law of the Old Testament (Mt 5:17); and he calls on animals to help him reveal meaning in the law that runs deeper than the letter. His call for "mercy, not sacrifice" (e.g., Mt 9:13) stands as an example; likewise, his eliminating the distinction between clean and unclean animals. In addition, to defend his decision to heal people on the Sabbath, Jesus asked his listeners, rhetorically, whether they would not save a sheep from a pit on the Sabbath (Mt 12:11), or lead a donkey or an ox to water (Lk 13:15), or save an ox from a well (Lk 14:5).

Life is more than food. The animals, which contribute much to Jesus's message, also are more than food. Our dietary choices are more than food, and as the early Christians demonstrated, the presence of the Holy Spirit in us gives us the freedom and the humility to reason through those choices.

18 MAN V. ANIMAL

Just as GOD concerned Himself at once with the people and the animals on the ark (Gen 8:1), and just as He concerned Himself at once with the people and the animals in Nineveh (Jonah 4:11), He concerns Himself at once with people and animals in other contexts as well, thereby highlighting our common needs or our compatible ways of life. For the most part, GOD intended humans and animals to live in harmony with each other. We ourselves have opportunities to fine-tune that harmony – for example, in contemplation of our health-maintenance practices.

Togetherness. In the Book of Jeremiah, GOD commands Jeremiah to disseminate a message of His support for Nebuchadnezzar, king of Babylon, whom He had allowed to lay siege to a disgraced Jerusalem. GOD prefaces His message with these words: "It is I who by my great power and my outstretched arm have made the earth, with the people and animals that are on the earth, and I give it to whomever I please" (Jer 27:5). In this verse, GOD presents both His human creation and His animal creation as testaments to His great power. Meanwhile, Psalm 104, quoted here and in chapter 1, captures some complementary rhythms in the lives of humans and animals:

You have made the moon to mark the seasons;
the sun knows its time for setting.
You make darkness, and it is night,
when all the animals of the forest come creeping out.
The young lions roar for their prey,
seeking their food from GOD.
When the sun rises, they withdraw
and lie down in their dens.
People go out to their work
and to their labor until the evening.

O LORD, how manifold are your works!
In wisdom you have made them all;
the earth is full of your creatures. (Ps 104:19-24)

In these verses, humans and animals follow each other in the dance of days, and all are integrated into the whole of GOD's Creation. The verse from Jeremiah suggests that the powers GOD tapped to create animals are on the same scale as the powers He tapped to create humans. Psalm 104 celebrates the intricacy of GOD's Design, the elaborate interplay between humans, animals, and the heavenly bodies. Humans and animals inhabit the earth together; they do not live worlds apart.

Shared Needs. On occasion, the Bible draws attention to humans' and animals' shared needs. In the Second Book of Kings, as the kings of Israel, Judah, and Edom sought to engage the Moabites in battle, they found themselves without a source of water. They asked the prophet Elisha to communicate with GOD about their predicament, and GOD gave Elisha this message: "You shall see neither wind nor rain, but the wadi shall be filled with water, so that you shall drink, you, your cattle, and your animals" (2Kings 3:17). In this episode, GOD plays the role of provider to humans and animals alike; He acknowledges the animals' needs along with the humans'.

Along the same lines, in the First Book of Kings, chapter 18, King Ahab sends Obadiah, a man of faith, on a mission to find grazing land for their animals. A drought had taken hold and had not let go for more than two years, and if any grass grew at all, it grew near springs or wadis. As Obadiah made his way in search of these oases, he encountered the prophet Elijah, whom GOD had sent to meet with King Ahab. Obadiah carried a message from Elijah to Ahab, and this brought about the meeting GOD desired.

Now, Ahab had turned many Israelites to Baal-worship, but Elijah helped to turn them back to GOD by making preparations for GOD to demonstrate His power where the invocations of Baal's so-called prophets failed. The false prophets were executed and GOD sent rain, as He promised He would. In this way, Obadiah's efforts to find grass for animals led to GOD's ending the drought, to the benefit of both people and animals.

As an aside, Obadiah's story is like Saul's in that by sending the men on their respective quests on animals' behalf, GOD led each to encounter a prophet. Saul's search for his father's donkeys ended with his meeting Samuel (1Sam 9:18-20); Obadiah's search ended with his meeting Elijah. In both cases, GOD must have known that He could rely on the men's concern for animals to help Him achieve His purpose.

In some passages of the Bible, the needs of animals coincide with the needs of children. On the warpath to Laish, the Danites put the children and the animals in front of them, presumably to protect them from threats such as the hostile, rear approach that soon materialized (Judg 18:21). When Jacob begged off travelling with Esau and his cohort, he said that both the "frail" children and the nursing mother animals would slow his pace (Gen 33:13-14). Fittingly, when Jacob died, the children and the animals were excused from making the long and arduous trek from Egypt to Canaan for his burial (Gen 50:8). Finally, according to some manuscripts, when Jesus questioned the Pharisees about the prohibition to work on the Sabbath, he asked them whether they wouldn't pull a child or an ox out of a well, if one fell in on the Sabbath (Lk 14:5) (and if the manuscripts are accurate, Jesus was not equating children with oxen when he spoke; rather, he was basing his comment on the fact that they would have had a similar need under the circumstances he described). The Bible presents these symmetries in a matter-of-fact way, and GOD expects us to appreciate them without reservation. He designed them, and as the verses above show, they allow us to discern, and thus to respond to, the needs of our animals, even as we attend to our own.

Healthy Common Sense. The Bible treats matters of health in a practical manner; the commonplace that sickness and disease imply suffering underlies many of the Bible's references to human health. GOD brings sickness as punishment (e.g., Ex 32:35; Rev 22:18) and protection from sickness as reward (e.g., Ex 23:25). In his first Epistle to the Corinthians, Paul writes that the body is a temple of the Holy Spirit (1Cor 6:19). While Paul writes this to discourage sexual immorality, the Spirit has inspired many Christians to generalize it and to apply it to their overall bodily health. The verses cited above and other verses support this generalization. John opens his third Epistle with a prayer for good health (3Jn 2), and Jesus blessed many with good health by means of his miraculous healings, which figured prominently in his ministry. All in all, the Bible presupposes that its readers desire good health and that that desire will inform their reading.

His Design Work Endures. Our health habits have the potential not only to improve our lives but also, writ large, to curb animal experimentation, intensive animal farming, and the destruction of animals' habitats. As to the first of these, animal experimentation has produced many health-related discoveries, but we probably could save more human lives by applying what we already know than by conducting further experiments. We know that a healthful diet, ample exercise, reduced stress levels, and personal and environmental cleanliness improve people's health; but, for various reasons, we sometimes fail to stick to these proactive strategies. If we were to shift our focus and our resources toward promoting these practices, we probably would enjoy better health; and we plausibly would curtail animal experimentation as a result. So, here, a scenario favorable to humans equates to a scenario favorable to animals as well.

In relation to diet, the overconsumption of animal products has been linked to killers such as cardiovascular disease and some cancers. By replacing some or all of the animal products in our diets with healthful, plant-based foods, many of us would be taking a step toward better health. This change also would benefit animals in that it would reduce demand for the products of intensive farming. In this way, once again, hopes for good health and goodwill toward animals complement each other.

Finally, animal farming produces food inefficiently, and this has implications for human health and for the preservation of animals' habitats. Farm animals consume multiple times more calories than they produce, and they account for the consumption of much water, including indirect consumption for the purposes of growing the food they eat, farm operations, transportation, etc. Land on which animal feed is grown would yield more calories for human consumption if its harvest went directly to humans. This would help to combat malnutrition among humans, especially the poor. It also would curtail the practice of destroying animals' natural habitats in order to create pastureland – a practice that defies GOD's will, mentioned in chapter 2 in connection with the Arabian ostrich, that birds and land animals of very kind abound on the earth (Gen 8:17); and a practice common in the meat-exporting Amazon region, where land-clearing burns sometimes even spread out of control and destroy more habitat than they otherwise would have.

To summarize, modifying our health-maintenance practices holds possibilities for alleviating suffering markedly among the less fortunate of us, and among wild animals besides. It also holds possibilities for cutting down on animal experimentation and intensive farming. Parallels between humans' being and animals' being show up unobtrusively in the Bible. GOD designed the world of animals to function in concert with ours, and His design work endures in phenomena like the positive repercussions our health-related choices can have for the animal world.

19 DOMINION III

In large part, chapter 3 examines the Bible's messages concerning dominion in the period before the Incarnation, and the subject of chapter 15 is the eternal dominion to be, after the Second Coming. This chapter looks at the period between those two times – that is, the period we are in now. The chapter draws much on the New Testament Epistles, which were written early in the present period. GOD fills His dominion over us with grace, mercy, and love. He has established this as the divine way, and the Bible guides us to go the way of GOD, however clumsily. We honor GOD by taking a caring approach, like His, to our exercise of dominion, and we reap spiritual benefits besides.

The Need for Grace, Mercy, and Love. Somebody somewhere probably has tallied the occurrences in the New Testament Epistles of the words "grace" and "gracious." The great number of occurrences reflects how very essential grace is to our continued engagement with GOD. We are justified by GOD's grace, through Jesus (Rom 3:24). Redemption and forgiveness derive from the grace that GOD has "lavished on us" (Eph 1:7-8). The hope expressed in the Gospels allows us truly to comprehend the grace of GOD (Col 1:3-6). GOD's grace leads us to moral behavior (2Cor 1:12). GOD bestowed His grace on us in the beginning, through Jesus (2Tim 1:9).

The Bible gives our reliance on GOD's mercy similar weight. Our sins beget GOD's mercy (Rom 11:32). GOD's mercy, through Christ, has effected our rebirth (1Pet 1:3). Mercy "triumphs over judgment" (Jas 2:13); and, to venture beyond the Epistles, "Blessed are the merciful, for they will receive mercy" (Mt 5:7).

Finally, our need for GOD's love might go the deepest of all. GOD is love (1Jn 4:16), and love has saved us (Jn 3:16). Love penetrates to the very identity of GOD, the Will behind all our blessings.

The Nature of Grace, Mercy, and Love. Grace, mercy, and love bloom directly from spirit; they are not predicated on any external factor. As to grace, Psalm 8 poses a question to GOD, below, that GOD later answers in the Book of Hebrews:

When I look at your heavens, the work of your fingers,
the moon and the stars that you have established;
What are human beings that you are mindful of them,
mortals that you care for them?

Yet you have made them a little lower than angels,
and crowned them with glory and honor.
You have given them dominion over the works of your hands;
you have put all things under their feet,
all sheep and oxen,
and also the beasts of the field,
the birds of the air, and the fish of the sea,
whatever passes along the paths of the seas. (Ps 8:3-8)

In the Book of Hebrews, GOD explains that the sense in which He has crowned us with glory and honor is that we have been brought to them through Jesus, whose suffering and death have redeemed us to Him (Heb 2:9-17). He writes that by His grace, Jesus has tasted death for everyone. As the Psalm implies, we ourselves have accomplished nothing that would merit the blessings GOD has given us. We have received them through grace. The Apostle Paul puts it succinctly in his Epistle to the Romans: "But if it is by grace, it is no longer on the basis of works, otherwise grace would no longer be grace" (Rom 11:6). Grace flows directly from the wellspring of spirit. It is not conditioned on works, it is given as a gift (2Cor 9:13-15).

Mercy and love are movements of the same symphony as grace. In the Book of Exodus, GOD tells Moses that He will be gracious and merciful to whomever He chooses (Ex 33:19). Paul comments on this in his Epistle to the Romans, writing, "So it depends not on human will or exertion, but on GOD, who shows mercy" (Rom 9:16). Of love, Paul writes that it is a fruit of the Holy Spirit (Gal 5:22) and that it never ends (1Cor 13:8). Jesus teaches us to love even our enemies (Mt 5:44), and we should beware any force that might diminish love's brilliance in us.

Be Imitators of GOD. The Bible exhorts us to emulate GOD's goodness. Paul instructs the Ephesians to imitate GOD (Eph 5:1), and the Corinthians to let all they do be done in love (1Cor 16:14). Jesus commands us to aspire to GOD's mercifulness (Lk 6:36) and perfection (Mt 5:48). John admonishes us to imitate what is good and not what is evil (3Jn 11), as does Paul (1Thes 5:21-22). And Peter reiterates GOD's command to the Israelites (Lev 19:2) to be holy because GOD is holy (1Pet 1:15-16).

Only through Christ can we attain these heights; without Christ as our Savior, GOD would reject our innately imperfect works. Nonetheless, apart from works, faith in Christ is dead (Jas 2:26), and GOD calls us to work for the good (Gal 6:7-10). The moral exercise of dominion is one way for us to do so.

The Bible promotes grace and mercy in our dominion via its predominantly accepting attitude toward animals, via its insistence on the moral treatment of animals, and via its accounts of and allusions to such treatment: from Noah's gentle handling of the dove (Gen 8:8-12); to Rebekah's watering Abraham's camels (Gen 24:14-19); to the then-blessed Saul's tireless search for his father's donkeys (1Sam 9:3-5); to the herder's allowing nursing mother animals to slow the pace of a drive (Gen 33:13-14); to the shepherd's seeking the lost, binding the wounded, healing the sick (Ezek 34:1-6), or laying down his life for his sheep (Jn 10:11-18); to Jesus's promising to send back the donkey that would carry him to his Triumphal Entry (Mk 11:3).

Also, regarding love, in the Second Book of Samuel, chapter 12, the prophet Nathan tells a story that features a human's love for an animal. With the story, Nathan dupes King David into passing judgment on himself for having committed adultery with Bethsheba, who was then the wife of Uriah the Hittite. Upon learning that Bethsheba had conceived his child, David summoned Uriah from the battlefield, where, as a soldier in David's army, he was participating in Israel's siege of the Ammonite city of Rabah. David schemed to reunite Uriah and Bethsheba, to create the appearance that Uriah had impregnated her; but Uriah evidently held to the soldier's age-old code of honor and refused to indulge in any of the comforts of home while his comrades remained in the field. David thereupon ordered Uriah's commander, Joab, to arrange for Uriah to be killed on the battlefield. Joab complied, and Uriah's death prompted GOD to send David a message through Nathan.

In the story Nathan told, below, the rich man represents David, the poor man Uriah, and the ewe Bethsheba. The wayfarer appears as a plot device:

And the LORD sent Nathan to David. He came to him and said to him, "There were two men in a certain city; the one rich and the other poor. The rich man had very many flocks and herds; but the poor man had nothing but one little ewe lamb, which he had bought. He brought it up, and it grew up with him and with his children; it used to eat of his meager fare, and drink from his cup, and lie in his bosom, and it was like a daughter to him. Now there came a traveler to the rich man, and he was loath to take one of his own flock or herd to prepare for the wayfarer who had come to him, but he took the poor man's lamb and prepared that for the guest who had come to him."
Then David's anger was greatly kindled against the man. He said to Nathan, "As the LORD lives, the man who has done this deserves to die; he shall restore the lamb fourfold, because he did this thing, and because he had no pity." (2Sam 12:1-6)

Whereupon Nathan said to David, "You are the man!" Nathan knew that David – and, ultimately, readers of the Bible – would recoil at the rich man's arrogance. Nathan's sympathetic portrayal of the poor man's relationship with the ewe amplifies the rich man's depravity. Nathan's story implicitly condones love for animals, and it warms the waters for us to love them now, as then.

Grace upon Grace. GOD is rich in mercy (Eph 2:4-5). Through love, GOD has made us His children (1Jn 3:1). From Jesus, we have received "grace upon grace" (Jn 1:16). As noted in chapter 15, in our dominion over animals, GOD does not require of us the level of selflessness that He has exhibited in His dominion over us. GOD's deciding to bless us with His grace, His mercy, and His love implied that He would have to offer His only begotten Son as a sacrifice; that, in obedience, His Son would have to go willingly to the altar of sacrifice; and that the Holy Spirit would have to take on a humble role as a sort of constant attendant to us (Jn 14:26).

On the other hand, our granting grace, mercy, and love to animals gives us blessed opportunities to move closer to GOD. Playing a part analogous to His gives us an opportunity to connect with Him and to gain insight into His nature. Playing a part analogous to His gives us an opportunity to see more clearly that His perfection is absolute, for we cannot improve upon His model of dominion.

These spiritual benefits stack grace upon the grace of GOD's dominion, yet more layers await. The moral exercise of dominion affords us other opportunities to deepen our relationship with GOD, and it aids us in our efforts to lead others to Him.

Animals transcend annuities. We should avoid idolizing them, but at the same time, we should avoid minimizing their importance. In relation to our treatment of them, questionable practices have been documented in print, on visual media, and online. Typically, profit motives drive these practices. However, if we allow them to, animals will serve us in infinitely longer-lasting ways, helping us to build treasures in heaven, which outshine nickels and dimes.

The Proper Role of Animals. In the Book of Job, Elihu offers the following commentary on opportunistic supplication to GOD:

"Because of the multitude of oppressions, people cry out;
they call for help because of the arm of the mighty.
But no one says, 'Where is GOD my Maker,
who gives strength in the night,
who teaches us more than the animals of the earth,
and makes us wiser than the birds of the air?'" (Job 35:9-11)

In this passage, Elihu decries the practice of praying to GOD in reactionary and shallow ways. GOD has more to offer than relief from the crisis of the moment, "the multitude of oppressions;" for example, He offers "strength in the night" and profound wisdom. As to the latter, Elihu brings animals into his speech to bring out GOD's supremacy. Animals sometimes impart wisdom. GOD always imparts more.

If, as we read and interpret the Bible, we look no higher than the level of animals, we risk idolatry, a greater regard for animals than for GOD. We would err by disdaining Balaam's mistreatment of his donkey but failing to see that greed had blinded him (Num 22). We would err by cheering the demise of animal sacrifice but conducting without integrity our relationship with GOD. We would err by estimating animals' earthly advantages to us but ignoring the standards of GOD's dominion over us.

Animals' greatest service to us is to point us in the direction of GOD – both His Person and His ways. Animals testify to His boundless wisdom, power, and creativity. In the Bible, they march us toward industry, they fly us toward faith, they carry us toward humility, they cry for our compassion, and they submit to our will. The Bible continues to edify us with its animals, and GOD continues to challenge us with the decision-making demands He has built into our relationship with them.

Christian Roles. In some settings, animals have been reduced to their economic value. Many aspects of these animals' lives have been subordinated to the bottom line: for example, access to the outdoors, access to fresh water, population density, allowance for movement, food and method of feeding, interactions with other animals of their kind, veterinary care, pain relief, etc. The incentivizing money comes from consumers, and a next step for Christians who have read this far would be to examine their own purchasing decisions.

To the extent that any changes we make bring hardship on people whose livelihoods depend on animals, we should engage with them proactively and with generosity. We should reinvigorate our ministerial efforts toward them, and, in another example of the parallels between the needs of humans and the needs of animals, our efforts may take on the added dimension of providing counsel on the godly treatment of animals, to the benefit of all.

Treasures in Heaven. The following passage is addressed to royalty or others who own flocks or herds and have delegated their day-to-day care to hired help:

Know well the condition of your flocks,
and give attention to your herds;
for riches do not last forever,
nor a crown for all generations.
When the grass is gone and new growth appears,
and the herbage of the mountain is gathered,
the lambs will provide your clothing,
and the goats the price of a field;
there will be enough goats' milk for your food,
for the food of your household
and nourishment for your servant-girls. (Prov 27:23-27)

This Proverb begins with the verse, "Do not boast about tomorrow, for you do not know what a day may bring" (Prov 27:1). Verses 23-27, above, direct owners to ensure that their animals are being cared for well, in case the owners' fortunes turn and they find themselves relying on lambswool or lambskin, goat's milk, and a single field. The second verse of the excerpt, lines 3 and 4, presages a teaching of Jesus's on the ephemeral nature of earthly wealth:

"Do not store up for yourselves treasures on earth, where moth and rust consume and where thieves break in and steal; but store up for yourselves treasures in heaven, where neither moth nor rust consumes and where thieves do not break in and steal. For where your treasure is, there your heart will be also." (Mt 6:19-21)

In addition to this, the Proverb as a whole also brings to mind Jesus's lessons that we cannot serve both GOD and wealth and that GOD will provide for us (Mt 6:24-33). The herd or the flock of the Proverb would keep faithful owners aware that they maintained but a tenuous hold on their riches. As a consequence, instead of serving their wealth, they would beware it, knowing that it might abandon them at any time. Meanwhile, the presence of the animals would reassure faithful owners that they could fall back on a simpler way of life, that GOD would provide, and that, like the lilies of the field and the birds of the air, they had no need to worry about what they would wear or what they would eat.

To sum up, the Proverb packs in its verses several recurrent themes. While animals have economic value, they matter more than money. People of faith nurture them. The Proverbs' animals point us toward GOD, fostering in us morals such as faith and humility. Moreover, the Proverb anticipates the New Testament and Christ's teachings, and the animals in it contribute to this synergy.

There is room in our embrace for both people and animals. Whereas people require our ongoing efforts at outreach and ministry, animals may enjoy lasting benefits from our making onetime lifestyle changes, changes that fast become second nature to us. GOD the Creator has blessed us with the animals. As long as our eyes are open, the animals will continue to reveal His glory to us. By working to treat animals in His way, we may gain a greater appreciation of the goodness He shows us, His underlings, whom He has immersed in kindness, compassion, grace, mercy, and love. A greater appreciation of GOD's goodness would add to the treasures we have accumulated in heaven, and to that end, the Holy Spirit may steer us toward a reexamination of our relationship with the animals. In the Book of Ecclesiastes, Solomon writes, "Guard your steps when you go to the House of GOD; to draw near to listen is better than the sacrifice offered by fools" (Ecc 5:1). If we draw near, we might hear in the coo of the Dove a call to greater goodness and to the LORD, our GOD of goodness without end.

APPENDIX I: SAMPLE RECIPES

The Value of Animals quotes or alludes to many Bible verses that might inspire you to adopt a plant-based diet. If you resolve to adopt one, work with an M.D. or a certified nutritionist who will take your goals seriously and who acknowledges that a considerable number of ordinary people have adopted a plant-based diet with no ill effects and with a number of good effects.

The recipes in this appendix are too few to represent the variety of dishes that the vegan diet offers. The recipes highlight some of the ingredients and methods characteristic of vegan cooking. The internet is replete with vegan recipes, and many specialty, vegan cookbooks have been published, which contain some of the best recipes of all. The internet also is a good resource for researching food ingredients.

Beans and Other Legumes • *Lentil Soup* • *Hot & Hearty Chili with Corn Bread* • *Curried Mushrooms & Garbanzo Beans, with Apple Chutney* • *Easy Pineapple Baked Beans* • *Sweet Potato & Black Bean Wraps* • *Whipped Garbanzo Wraps*
Textured Vegetable Protein (TVP) • *Tacos* • *Sloppy Joes*
Tofu • *Tofu & Vegetable Stir Fry* • *Stroganoff* • *Crumble Coffee Cake* • *Cookies & Peanut Butter Cream*
Tempeh • *Tempeh & Wild Rice Casserole* • *Simple BBQ Tempeh Wraps*
Egg Replacer • *Breaded Eggplant Sandwiches* • *Bran Muffins*
Traditional Ingredients • *Pasta in Traditional Italian Sauce* • *Potato Gnocchi in Spicy Sauce* • *Corn Chowder* • *Oat Patties* • *Rice Loaf* • *Bread Dressing* • *Grilled Portobello Mushrooms or Summertime Variety* • *Whole Wheat Banana Pancakes* • *Banana Cake* • *Carob & Peanut Butter Smoothie* • *Simple Chocolate Cake*
Other Suggesions

BEANS AND OTHER LEGUMES
Beans and other legumes are a major part of the typical plant-based diet, contributing much heartiness and flavor to it.

LENTIL SOUP

2 cups dry lentils
4 cups vegetable broth
One 28 oz. can stewed tomatoes
2 tablespoons lemon juice
chopped carrot, celery, and onion – to make a hearty soup
2 teaspoons thyme
2 bay leaves

o In a large pot, cook the lentils according to package directions, being careful not to overcook them. Drain the cooked lentils and return them to the pot.
o Stir in the stewed tomatoes with their liquid, along with all the remaining ingredients except the bay leaves.
o Add the bay leaves, bring the soup to a boil, reduce the heat, and simmer until the vegetables are tender.
o Remove the bay leaves, and serve the soup hot.

Serves 6

HOT & HEARTY CHILI, WITH CORN BREAD

Corn Bread

1 cup cornmeal

1 cup unbleached all-purpose flour
2 teaspoons reduced-sodium baking powder
2 teaspoons sugar
1 teaspoon salt
2 tablespoons oil
1 ½ cups soy milk or other vegan milk

Preheat the oven to 350 degrees.
o In a large bowl, stir together the five dry ingredients. Add the oil and the vegan milk and stir thoroughly.
o Pour the batter into a lightly oiled 8-inch x 8-inch pan. Bake at 350 degrees for 30 minutes. Serve warm, with the chili.

Chili

2 tablespoons vegetable oil
1 onion, chopped
5 cloves minced garlic
1 green bell pepper, seeded and chopped
1 red bell pepper, seeded and chopped
1 habanero pepper, seeded and minced
1 jalapeno pepper, seeded and minced
2 tablespoons chili powder
1 tablespoon red pepper flakes
1 tablespoon paprika
1 tablespoon cumin
2 teaspoons oregano
1 tablespoon freshly ground black pepper
2 teaspoons seasoned salt
1 tablespoon cocoa powder
two 14.5 oz. cans diced tomato with green chile peppers, drained
one 8 oz. can tomato sauce
one 15 oz. can kidney beans, drained and rinsed
½ cup beer OR ¼ cup water
1 tablespoon liquid smoke flavoring
3 tablespoons sugar
1 tablespoon hot pepper sauce
12-16 oz. frozen vegan ground-beef substitute
1 cup frozen corn kernels

o In a large pot, sauté the onion, garlic, and peppers in the oil, until the onion begins to soften.
o Stirring constantly, add the spices, the black pepper, the seasoned salt, and the cocoa.
o Add all the remaining ingredients except the beef substitute and the corn. Stir well to diffuse the spices.
o Add the beef substitute and the corn, bring the chili to a simmer and simmer for 30 minutes. Serve hot.

Serves 6

CURRIED MUSHROOMS & GARBANZO BEANS, WITH APPLE CHUTNEY
The apple chutney portion of this recipe makes a good accompaniment to many curries; nevertheless, chopped apples are a satisfying and expeditious alternative.

Apple Chutney

2 pounds dense apples, peeled and chopped
1 cup cider vinegar

1 cup sugar
3 tablespoons minced garlic
2 teaspoons each of ginger powder, ground cinnamon, and ground cloves
½ cup orange juice
½ teaspoon cayenne powder

o Stir all the ingredients together in a pot. Bring to a simmer and cook uncovered, stirring occasionally, for about half an hour – until most of the liquid has been absorbed and the chutney has the consistency of fruit preserves. To hasten the process, increase the heat and stir frequently. Allow the chutney to cool before serving, and refrigerate or freeze any unused portions.

Makes 12 side servings

Curry

1 tablespoon vegetable oil
1 large onion, chopped
1 ½ pounds sliced, fresh mushrooms
1 ½ tablespoons whole cumin seeds
one 28 oz. can crushed tomatoes
one 15 oz. can garbanzo beans, drained and rinsed
1 teaspoon turmeric
1 teaspoon coriander
1 teaspoon cayenne
½ teaspoon ginger

o In a large pot, sauté the onion in the oil until it begins to soften. Add the cumin seeds and the mushrooms, and stir and cook until the mushrooms are browned.
o Stir in the remaining ingredients and simmer for 30 minutes.
Serve hot over hot, cooked basmati rice, with the prepared chutney or chopped apples, and with naan or pita bread.

Serves 4-6

EASY PINEAPPLE BAKED BEANS

one 28 oz. can vegetarian baked beans
one 8 oz. can diced pineapple, drained
1 small onion, diced
1 small green pepper, seeded and diced
2 teaspoons reduced-sodium soy sauce
hot, cooked brown rice

o In a large pot, sauté the onion and green pepper in a little oil until they begin to soften. Add the remaining ingredients and heat through, uncovered.
Serve hot over the hot rice.

Serves 4-5

SWEET POTATO & BLACK BEAN WRAPS

1 medium sweet potato, washed, peeled and cut into small cubes
2 cups hot, cooked brown rice
one 12 oz. can black beans, drained, rinsed, and warmed
2 ½ teaspoons curry powder
⅛ teaspoon cayenne powder
lard-free, enchilada-size corn tortillas

salsa
plain soy yogurt

o Steam the sweet potato cubes until soft.
o Gently stir together the potatoes, the rice, and the beans.
o Sprinkle this mixture with the spices and stir again, to diffuse them.
o Spoon some salsa onto the centers of the tortillas and spoon the bean mixture on top of it.
Roll the tortillas and serve warm. Dip in the soy yogurt.

Serves 3-4

WHIPPED GARBANZO WRAPS

two 15 oz. cans garbanzo beans
1 teaspoon garlic powder
2 tablespoons reduced-sodium soy sauce
6 tablespoons olive oil
2 tablespoons lemon juice
freshly ground black pepper
lard-free, flour burrito tortillas
1 small red bell pepper, seeded and cut into strips
1 small green bell pepper, seeded and cut into strips
1 small red onion, halved and sliced

o Drain the garbanzo beans, reserving the liquid. Place the first six ingredients in a food processor and blend until smooth. With the food processor running, slowly add the reserved liquid through the feeder opening, until the mixture takes on a fluffy consistency.
o Place the bell pepper and onion strips on the centers of the tortillas. Spoon the garbanzo mixture on the vegetables and fold the tortillas burrito-style.
o Over medium heat, brown the top and bottom surfaces of the wraps on an ungreased skillet or griddle.
Serve warm.

Serves 4

TEXTURED VEGETABLE PROTEIN (TVP)

Textured vegetable protein is made of the flour that is left over after the oil is extracted from legumes – often, soy beans. Dry TVP flakes may be stored in the pantry and used in a variety of recipes. The taco and sloppy joe recipes below show how convenient and quick-to-cook it is.

TACOS

1 cup water
1 small onion, diced
1 small red pepper, diced
2 garlic cloves, crushed
¾ cup TVP
1 cup tomato sauce
2 teaspoons chili powder
½ teaspoon cumin
¼ teaspoon oregano
1 tablespoon nutritional yeast
1 tablespoon reduced-sodium soy sauce
lard-free soft taco tortillas

o In a large saucepan, cook the onion and red pepper in a little of the water, until the onion is soft. Stir in all the remaining ingredients except the tortillas, and heat through, uncovered. Stir in just enough additional TVP to absorb any excess liquid.

o Spoon some of the hot mixture onto one half of a tortilla. Fold the tortilla in half over the filling, and brown each side on an ungreased skillet. Keep warm and repeat with the remaining tortillas.

Serve hot or warm with your favorite taco toppings.

Serves 4-6

SLOPPY JOES

1½ cups water
1 small onion, diced
1 small red pepper, diced
1 cup TVP
one 15 oz. can tomato sauce
1 tablespoon sugar
1 teaspoon chili powder
1 teaspoon garlic powder
2 tablespoons cider vinegar
1 teaspoon reduced-sodium soy sauce
1 teaspoon Dijon mustard

o In a large saucepan, cook the onion and red pepper in a little of the water, until the onion is soft.

o Stir in all the remaining ingredients and heat through, uncovered. Stir in just enough additional TVP to absorb any excess liquid.

Serve hot on burger buns.

Serves 4-6

TOFU

Tofu comes in firm, extra firm, and silken varieties. Because it contains proportionally less water than the other varieties, extra firm tofu crisps the best and is well suited for recipes like the stir fry recipe below. Silken tofu is a good binding agent and is well suited for recipes like the coffee cake recipe below. When it is blended, silken tofu gives recipes a creamy consistency, and its mild flavor yields to the flavors of other ingredients, as in the stroganoff and peanut butter cream recipes.

TOFU AND VEGETABLE STIR FRY

Sauce
¾ cup vegetable broth
¼ cup reduced-sodium soy sauce
2-3 tablespoons brown sugar
2 teaspoons cornstarch
1 teaspoon red pepper flakes

Stir Fry
14 ounces extra firm tofu, drained
the florets of one medium head of broccoli
1 medium red bell pepper, seeded and sliced
1 medium carrot, julienned
1 onion, quartered and sliced
4 cloves garlic, minced
2 tablespoons fresh, minced ginger root

o *Optional:* To press some of the moisture out of the tofu, wrap it in a towel and place a book or other weighty object on it for a few minutes.

o In a sealable bowl, whisk together all of the sauce ingredients, cover, and set aside.

o Cut the tofu into medium-size cubes and toss the cubes in the cornstarch.

o To a wok or a frying pan, add enough vegetable oil to cover the bottom of it. Heat the oil and then add the tofu cubes in a single layer.

o Cook the tofu over medium-high heat, turning each cube until each of its sides is golden brown. Remove and set aside.

o Add a little oil to the cooking surface and when it's hot, add the garlic and ginger. Cook until the ginger is aromatic.

o Add the vegetables and stir fry over high heat until they are just tender.

o Add the sauce to the pan, stir and cook until the sauce begins to thicken.

o Add the tofu, stir, and heat through.

Serve hot either on its own or over hot noodles or rice.

STROGANOFF

1 twelve-ounce package silken tofu
1 tablespoon lemon juice
½ cup white wine OR ⅓ cup grape juice and 3 tablespoons water
1 medium onion, chopped
3 cloves of garlic, minced
1 pound fresh, sliced mushrooms
1 tablespoon paprika
2 tablespoons reduced-sodium soy sauce
2 tablespoons Dijon mustard
3 tablespoons unbleached all-purpose flour
freshly ground black pepper, to taste

o In a blender or small food processor, blend the tofu and lemon juice.
o In a large saucepan, sauté the onion and garlic in a little oil, until the onion begins to soften
o Add the wine OR the grape juice and water. Add the mushrooms, cover, and cook until warm.
o Sprinkle in the paprika, add the mustard and soy sauce, and stir well.
o Slowly sprinkle in the flour, stirring constantly, until a smooth paste forms.
o Stir in the tofu mixture and pepper, and cook until heated through.
Serve hot over hot, cooked pasta or rice, or over toast.

Serves 6

CRUMBLE COFFE CAKE
In this recipe, walnuts chopped thoroughly in a food processor produce the best results.

1 cup soy milk or other vegan milk
1 tablespoon vinegar
⅓ cup silken tofu
2 ¼ cups whole wheat flour
1 ¼ cups sugar
3 teaspoons ground cinnamon (2 ½ & ½)

1 ½ teaspoons ground ginger
½ teaspoon salt
½ cup vegetable oil
¾ cup very finely chopped walnuts
1 teaspoon reduced-sodium baking powder
1 teaspoon baking soda

Preheat the oven to 350 degrees
o In a blender, blend the vegan milk, the vinegar, and the tofu until smooth.
o In a large bowl, stir together the flour, the sugar, the ginger, the salt, the oil, and 2½ teaspoons of the cinnamon. With a fork or your fingers, work this mixture until it has a moist and crumbly consistency.
o In a smaller bowl, make the streusel topping by stirring together 1¼ cups of the flour mixture, the walnuts, and the rest of the cinnamon (½ t).
o To the flour mixture in the larger bowl, add the baking powder, the baking soda, and the blended tofu mixture. Mix until smooth and pour into a lightly oiled 9-inch x 13-inch baking dish. Sprinkle the streusel topping on the batter.
o Bake at 350 degrees for 30 to 35 minutes, until a toothpick inserted into the center comes out clean. Remove from the oven and allow the cake to cool before slicing and serving.

Serves 8

COOKIES AND PEANUT BUTTER CREAM
As of this writing, some national brands of chocolate sandwich cookies are entirely plant-based.

18 vegan chocolate sandwich cookies, unstacked
one 12 oz. cake of silken tofu
1 cup creamy peanut butter, softened
½ cup sugar
2 teaspoons vanilla extract

o Chop the cookies in a food processor. Empty them into a bowl and set aside.
o Place the remaining ingredients in the food processor and blend until smooth.
o Spoon the peanut butter mixture into small bowls and cover with the chopped cookies. Chill and serve.

Serves 4-6

TEMPEH

Tempeh is another versatile, soybean product, with a meaty texture. In the recipes below, it is interchangeable with commercial, chicken-style vegan strips, which are less widely available than tempeh.

TEMPEH AND WILD-RICE CASSEROLE
This casserole is a vegan adaptation of a popular chicken casserole.
As of this writing, some national brands of onion soup mix and seasoned wild rice are entirely plant-based.

Sauce

1 medium onion, diced
¼ cup unbleached all-purpose flour
1 ½ tablespoons poultry seasoning
2 cups hot vegetable broth
½ cup diced, fresh or canned mushrooms
3 tablespoons nutritional yeast

o In a saucepan, sauté the onion in a little oil until it begins to soften.
o Add the flour and the poultry seasoning, and stir to coat.

o Add the vegetable broth, stirring constantly.
o Add the mushrooms and yeast, and stir until the sauce thickens.
o Remove from heat and set aside.

Casserole

two 4-4.5 oz. boxes long grain and wild rice, with their seasoning packets
1 envelope onion soup mix
8 oz. tempeh, cut into strips
12 oz. vegetable broth
¾ cup water

Preheat the oven to 350 degrees.
o In a 9 x 13 baking dish, mix together the rice, the seasoning, and the soup mix. Spread the mixture evenly over the bottom of the dish.
o Arrange the tempeh evenly on top of the rice, and pour in the broth and water.
o Pour the prepared sauce evenly over the rice. Cover tightly with foil and bake at 350 degrees for 30 minutes. Remove the foil and bake for an additional 30 minutes.
Serve hot, with cranberry sauce.

Serves 6

SIMPLE BBQ TEMPEH WRAPS
As of this writing, some national brands of barbeque sauce are entirely plant-based.

1 medium red or yellow bell pepper, cut into strips
1 small onion, halved and sliced
8 oz. tempeh, cut into strips
prepared, vegan barbeque sauce
lard-free fajita tortillas
prepared salsa

o Sauté the pepper and onion in a little vegetable oil, until they begin to soften.
o Add the tempeh and barbeque sauce to taste, and heat through.
o Spoon some salsa on the centers of the tortillas, top with the tempeh filling, and wrap burrito-style. Serve hot.

Serves 4

EGG REPLACER

Commercial egg replacer comes in powdered and liquid forms. Other plant-based ingredients moisturize and bind -- for example, the tofu in the coffee cake recipe above, and the bananas in the pancake and cake recipes below -- but commercial egg replacers work best as an initial replacement in recipes that call for eggs. Commercial egg replacers most reliably mimic the binding, moisturizing, and leavening effects of eggs.

BREADED EGGPLANT SANDWICHES

1 medium eggplant, peeled
½ cup vegan milk
egg replacer equivalent of 2 eggs
unbleached all-purpose flour
Italian-style bread crumbs
sub buns, toasted
marinara sauce

Preheat the oven to 400 degrees.

o Cut the eggplant lengthwise into broad, ½-inch-thick slices
o If using powdered egg replacer, dissolve it according to package directions, in hot water if the directions allow for it.
o Mix the egg replacer well with the vegan milk. Pour the mixture into a shallow pan or pie tin.
o Pour some flour into a second shallow pan or pie tin and dredge a slice of the eggplant through it, until covered.
o Submerge the eggplant in the vegan milk mixture, remove, and shake off the excess.
o Sprinkle both sides of the eggplant with bread crumbs, until covered.
o Place the eggplant on a lightly greased baking sheet.
o Repeat with the remaining slices
o Bake at 400 degrees for 15 to 20 minutes. Remove from the oven, place the baked eggplant in the sub buns, and top with hot marinara sauce.
Serve hot.

BRAN MUFFINS

egg replacer equivalent of 4 eggs
3 cups sugar
3 teaspoons salt
5 cups whole wheat flour
1 cup vegetable oil
2 cups warm water
one 22 oz. box bran nuggets cereal
1 quart warm soy milk or other vegan milk, with 5 teaspoons baking soda stirred into it

o If using powdered egg replacer, dissolve it according to package directions, in hot water if the directions allow for it.
o In a very large bowl, add the ingredients in the order listed, stirring with each addition. Cover the batter and refrigerate overnight.

Preheat the oven to 350 degrees.
o Mix the batter with a power mixture until smooth.
o Spoon the batter into oiled muffin tins, filling each about three-fourths full.
o Bake for about 30 minutes, until a toothpick inserted into the center of a muffin comes out clean.
Cover and refrigerate any unused batter for as many as four days.

Makes 3-4 dozen muffins

TRADITIONAL INGREDIENTS

Plant-based diets rely primarily on common ingredients. The recipes below feature tomatoes, potatoes, oats and rice, mushrooms, bananas, and other common ingredients.

PASTA IN TRADITIONAL ITALIAN SAUCE

¼ cup olive oil
1 medium onion, chopped
1 small red bell pepper, finely chopped
8 cloves garlic, minced
½ pound sliced, fresh mushrooms
1 cup red wine OR ½ cup grape juice
two 28 oz cans crushed plum tomatoes
12 ounces tomato paste
1 tablespoon minced fresh basil
1 tablespoon minced fresh parsley
1 tablespoon minced fresh oregano
1 teaspoon dried thyme

1 teaspoon crumbled sage
1 teaspoon dried rosemary
2 tablespoons sugar, if using wine
3 bay leaves

○ Heat the oil in a large pot. Add the onion, red pepper, garlic, and mushrooms, and sauté until the onion is tender.
○ If using wine, add it and cook until it is reduced by about half.
○ Stir in all the remaining ingredients and bring the sauce to a boil. Reduce the heat, cover, and simmer for an hour, stirring occasionally.
○ Uncover and continue to simmer, stirring frequently, until the sauce has thickened.
Serve hot, over hot, cooked pasta.

Serves 8

POTATO GNOCCHI in SPICY SAUCE
This combination recipe comprises the second of two tomato-based recipes and the first of two potato-based recipes. When you prepare the gnocchi, leave enough time for the potatoes to cool, lest the dough be too hot to handle.

Gnocchi

1 ½ pounds Yukon Gold or Russet potatoes – washed, peeled, sliced, and steamed or boiled until soft
1 ½ cups unbleached all-purpose flour
1 tablespoon olive oil

○ Drain the potatoes (if boiled). Allow the potatoes to cool before proceeding. In a large bowl, mash the potatoes without adding any liquid to them. Stir in the flour and oil. Knead the resulting dough until it is smooth, adding flour in small increments if it is sticky.
○ Divide the dough into quarters, and on a flour-dusted surface, roll each quarter into a cylinder about ¾ inch in diameter. Slice each cylinder into bite-size segments. Lightly press the tips of your pinkie fingers into the flat sides of each segment, to create dimples in it.
○ Bring a pot of water to a boil and drop some of the gnocchi into it. Boil for 2-3 minutes or so, until the gnocchi rises to the surface of the water. Drain, or remove with a slotted spoon. Repeat with the remaining dumplings.
Serve hot, with the sauce.

Sauce

2 tablespoons olive oil
½ teaspoon salt
4 cloves of garlic, minced
2 teaspoons oregano
10 leaves fresh basil, chopped, or 1 tablespoon dried basil
1 teaspoon hot pepper flakes
one 28 oz. can whole peeled tomatoes with liquid

○ In a saucepan, heat the oil. Add the garlic and sauté until it begins to brown. Add all the other ingredients and stir well. Simmer the sauce, uncovered, until it thickens, stirring occasionally and breaking up the tomatoes as they cook.

Serves 4

CORN CHOWDER

3 medium potatoes, washed, chopped, and steamed or boiled until soft
½ cup soy milk or other vegan milk
vegetable broth

2 teaspoons oil
1 small onion, finely chopped
1 stalk celery, diced
1 medium carrot, diced
1 small red bell pepper, seeded and diced
1 cup frozen corn kernels

○ Drain the potatoes, if boiled. In a blender, blend the potatoes, the vegan milk, and just enough broth to give the chowder a thick and creamy consistency.
○ Sauté the onion, celery, carrot, and bell pepper in the oil until just tender.
○ Pour the chowder into a pot and stir in the cooked vegetables and the corn. Without boiling it, heat the chowder until the corn is hot.
Serve hot.

Serves 4-6

OAT PATTIES

4 cups cooked and cooled oatmeal
1 medium onion, pureed
2 teaspoons oregano
1 teaspoon black pepper

Preheat the oven to 350 degrees.

○ In a large bowl, mix all the ingredients with a spoon, until the mixture binds. Form the mixture into patties and bake at 350 degrees for 30 minutes.
Serve hot on buns, with your favorite condiments.

Makes 5 or 6 patties

RICE LOAF

2 cups cooked and cooled brown rice
1 cup walnuts, finely chopped
1 cup diced mushrooms
1 small onion, diced
1 small red pepper, diced
1 carrot, shredded
1 cup wheat germ
1 cup rolled oats – instant or traditional – mixed with ½ cup hot tap water
½ teaspoon each marjoram, thyme, and sage
2 tablespoons reduced-sodium soy sauce
2 tablespoons stone ground or Dijon mustard
3 tablespoons sugar
ketchup or vegan barbeque sauce

Preheat the oven to 350 degrees.
○ Put all of the ingredients in a large bowl and mix with a large spoon for 2-4 minutes, until the mixture binds.
○ Spoon the mixture into a greased 5 x 9 loaf pan and press it down.
○ Top the loaf with ketchup or barbeque sauce, and bake at 350 degrees for 60 minutes
○ Remove the loaf from the oven, let it cool for 15 minutes or so, and then remove it from the pan and slice.
Serve hot, and top with ketchup, barbeque sauce, or a commercial or homemade vegan gravy.

Serves 6

BREAD DRESSING
Bread that is dense but not crusty suits this recipe best.

1 tablespoon vegetable oil
1 medium onion, chopped
1 ½ cup sliced, fresh mushrooms
2-3 celery stalks, sliced
6 cups bread, cut into small cubes
½ cup diced, fresh parsley
1 teaspoon thyme
1 teaspoon marjoram
1 teaspoon sage
¼ teaspoon ground black pepper
1 ½ cups steaming hot vegetable broth

Preheat the oven to 350 degrees
o In a large pot, sauté the onion in the oil until the onion begins to soften. Add the mushrooms and cook, stirring frequently, until the mushrooms begin to brown.
o Stir in the bread, celery, and spices, and then stir in the broth in small increments, until the dressing is moist. If needed, stir in some hot water to moisten further.
o Spoon the mixture into a lightly oiled baking dish. Bake covered at 350 degrees for 20 minutes. Remove the cover and bake for an additional 10 minutes.
Serve hot, as a side.

Serves 4-6

GRILLED PORTOBELLO MUSHROOMS OR SUMMERTIME VARIETY

Vegetables
6 portobello mushroom caps
OR
6 servings of in-season vegetables for the grill (zucchini, summer squash, button mushrooms, bell pepper, onion, cherry tomatoes, broccoli, etc.)

Marinade
½ cup reduced-sodium soy sauce
2 tablespoons liquid smoke
¼ cup vegetable oil
¼ cup lemon juice
2 tablespoons brown sugar
3 cloves garlic, crushed
freshly ground black pepper

In a bowl, mix all the marinade ingredients together. Pour the marinade into a pan and partially immerse in it the portobello caps, gills down, or the other vegetables, chopped and seeded as necessary. Refrigerate, uncovered, for two hours or more.

Portobello cap directions
o Place the mushroom caps directly on a hot grill, and spoon some of the remaining marinade on them, a little at a time, as they cook.
o Turn the caps after the first side begins to blacken.
o Continue to cook and turn the caps until they are heated through and moist but not running with juices.
Serve hot on sturdy buns, with your favorite toppings.

Vegetable variety directions

o Place the vegetables on skewers or in a grill basket, and then place them on a hot grill, spooning some of the remaining marinade on the vegetables, a little at a time, as they cook.

o If using skewers, turn the skewers after the first sides of the vegetables begin to blacken; if using a grill basket, stir the vegetables frequently.

Serve over hot rice or pasta. Heat any leftover marinade and drizzle it over the vegetables before eating.

Serves 6

WHOLE WHEAT BANANA PANCAKES

2 ripe bananas
2 ½ cups soy milk or other vegan milk
2 tablespoons maple syrup
2 cups whole wheat flour
4 teaspoons reduced-sodium baking powder
½ teaspoon salt
Chopped walnuts, optional

o Thoroughly mash the bananas in a large bowl, then stir in the vegan milk and the maple syrup.

o In a separate bowl, stir together the flour, baking soda, and salt. Add this to the banana mixture and stir until smooth.

o Pour ¼ cup of the batter into a preheated, lightly oiled skillet. Sprinkle with walnuts, if using.

o Cook until the top bubbles, turn with a spatula, and cook the second side.

o Keep warm and repeat with the remaining batter.

Serve hot or warm, with maple syrup or fruit compote.

BANANA CAKE
Whole grain flour is a good fit for this moist cake.

3 cups whole wheat flour
2 ¼ teaspoons baking soda
¾ teaspoon salt
1 ½ cups sugar
½ cup vegetable oil
6 ripe bananas, mashed (about 4 cups)
⅜ cup water
1 ½ teaspoons vanilla extract

Preheat the oven to 350 degrees.

o In a bowl, stir the flour, baking soda, and salt together.

o In a separate, large bowl, beat the sugar and oil together. Mix in the mashed bananas, water, and vanilla extract. Stir in the flour mixture, and spread the batter into a lightly oiled 9 x 13 baking dish.

o Bake at 350 degrees for about 50 minutes, until a toothpick inserted into the center comes out clean. Allow the cake to cool. Spread with a vegan frosting, slice, and serve (as of this writing, some national brands of frosting are entirely plant-based).

Serves 10

CAROB & PEANUT BUTTER SMOOTHIE
Be sure not to freeze the bananas in large clusters, as they would have to be broken up before blending – an arduous task.

3 tablespoons carob powder
3 medium bananas, diced and frozen in thin layers
⅓ cup creamy peanut butter, softened
2 tablespoons maple syrup
3 cups soy milk or other vegan milk

Place all the ingredients in a blender, in the order listed. Blend until smooth, pour into glasses, and serve promptly.

Serves 4

SIMPLE CHOCOLATE CAKE

2 ¼ cups unbleached all-purpose flour
1 ½ cups sugar
4 ½ tablespoons cocoa powder
1 ½ teaspoons baking soda
1 ½ teaspoons vanilla extract
1 ½ tablespoons distilled white vinegar
½ cup vegetable oil
1 ½ cups cold water

o Preheat the oven to 350 degrees.
o In a large bowl, stir together the flour, sugar, cocoa, and baking soda.
o Stir in the vanilla, vinegar, and oil
o Add the water and stir until the batter is smooth.
o Pour the batter into a lightly greased 9 x 13 baking dish
o Bake at 350 degrees for about 35 minutes, until a knife inserted into the center comes out clean.
Allow the cake to cool. Spread with a vegan frosting, slice, and serve (as of this writing, some national brands of frosting are entirely plant-based).

Serves 10

OTHER SUGGESTIONS
The internet is the best resource for other suggestions, but below, I've listed a few favorites that you might find there.

□ vegan dishes at local, ethnic restaurants
□ vegan convenience foods: microwaveable meals; burgers, hot dogs, imitation ground sausage, etc.
□ vegan dips and relishes, such as hummus, guacamole, black-eyed pea relish, and baba ghanoush
□ simple snack mix: three parts toasted oats cereal, and one part each raisins, semisweet chocolate chips, and peanuts
□ sandwiches...
    ◊ all-vegetable submarine sandwiches
    ◊ grilled vegan Reubens: rye bread, sauerkraut, mustard, eggless thousand-island dressing, and toppings of your choice (e.g., sliced tomato and avocado)
    ◊ vegan BLT's
    ◊ tomato, fresh basil, and vegan mayonnaise
    ◊ peanut butter and jelly
□ falafel
□ rice-based wraps: lard-free refried beans, leftovers, or vegetables and seasonings of your choice – combined with rice and wrapped in lard-free tortillas
□ prepared, commercial sauces: marinara, pesto, sweet-and-sour, curry, stir-fry, etc.
□ polenta
□ vegetable salads
□ fruit salads
□ easy parfait: layer granola, soy yogurt, and chopped, fresh fruit
□ breakfast cereal and vegan milk
□ fruit cobblers
□ fruit pies, with crusts made with vegetable shortening
□ vegan sorbet and ice cream

APPENDIX II: OTHER RELEVANT VERSES

CHAPTER 1 "GOD's Animals"

Exodus 11:7 - GOD considers the Israelite community to comprise both humans and animals, as in Jonah 4:9-11.

CHAPTER 2 "The Living Word"

Hebrews 12:20 - GOD calls on the hapless, at-risk animals of Exodus 19:12-13 to help Him paint the contrast between the Mount Sinai of the Old Covenant and the Mount Zion of the New.
Isaiah 14:11 - Another verse made memorable by its allusion to the animal realm. "Your pomp is brought down to Sheol, / and the sound of your harps; / maggots are the bed beneath you, / and worms are your covering."
Jeremiah 46:20 - As above. "A beautiful heifer is Egypt – a gadfly from the north lights upon her."
Job 8:13-14 - As above. "Such are the paths of all who forget GOD; / the hope of the godless shall perish. / Their confidence is gossamer, / a spider's house their trust."
Psalm 102:6-7 - As above. "I am like an owl of the wilderness, / like a little owl of the waste places. / I lie awake; / I am like a lonely bird on the housetop."
Psalm 140:3 - As above. "They make their tongue sharp as a snake's, / and under their lips is the venom of vipers."

CHAPTER 3 "Dominion I"

1Kings 4:24-25 - A description of Solomon's dominion, one of peace.
Psalm 145:13 - A fine description of GOD's dominion. "Your kingdom is an everlasting kingdom, / and your dominion endures throughout all generations. / The LORD is faithful in all His words, / and gracious in all His deeds."

CHAPTER 4 "Suffering; Sacrifice"

Amos 5:21-24 - Another commentary on the corruption of sacrificial and other rites. GOD will not accept sacrifices; He desires justice and righteousness.
Deuteronomy 21:1-9 - The procedure established to address unsolved murders involves breaking a heifer's neck, reminiscent of Exodus 13:13.
Ezekiel 39:17-20 - GOD commands Ezekiel to extend to the wild animals an ironic invitation to attend a sacrificial feast, at which they will eat the flesh and drink the blood of Israel's enemies and their animals.
Genesis 15:7-21 - Abram cuts three animal carcasses in half, and in the form of a fire pot and a torch, GOD ceremonially passes between the halves, thus making a covenant with Abram.
Hosea 8:11 - Another commentary on the corruption of sacrificial rites: Ephraim's proliferation of altars is described as a tribute to sin.
Jeremiah 34:18-19 - This is another example of the covenant ceremony depicted in Genesis 15:7-21, above.
Matthew 18:6-7 - Jesus uses the stumbling block as a symbol of an impediment to faith.
Psalm 27:6 - "...and I will offer in His tent / sacrifices with shouts of joy; / I will sing and make melody to the LORD." Similar to Psalm 51:15-19
Psalm 50:13-14 - "Do I eat the flesh of bulls / or drink the blood of goats? / Offer to GOD a sacrifice of thanksgiving, / and pay your vows to the Most High." Similar to Psalm 69:30-33.
1Samuel 17:34-35 - David relates his shepherding exploits in which he saved lambs from predators' mouths, killing the predators if they turned on him. Reminiscent of Judges 14:6.

CHAPTER 5. "Economics"

Deuteronomy 4:15-18 - GOD explains that idols cannot represent Him, because He is formless.
1Kings 10:22 - In describing the opulence of Solomon's reign, the Bible mentions that once every three years ships would convey ivory, apes, and peacocks to Israel. The Bible indicates neither how many animals

were involved nor how they were treated. Given Solomon's appreciation for animals (1Kings 4:29-34), they probably were treated humanely.

Revelation 18:2 - Unlike Ezekiel 8:9-10, which attacks idols fashioned as animals, Revelation 18:2's description of birds and beasts as "foul" and "hateful" applies directly to the animals themselves. Revelation 18:2 is prophesied by Jeremiah, who writes of Babylon's being inhabited by hyenas and ostriches (Jer 50:39); and it is prophesied by Isaiah, who adds jackals to the list (Isa 13:19-22). GOD sometimes looks askance at these three creations of His. The Bible mentions the cruelty of the ostrich multiple times, and it presents the lairs of jackals as sinister places (e.g., Jer 9:11). Each of these animals emits one or more unearthly sounds. The ostrich and the hyena laugh; the "booming" ostrich and the wailing jackal make sounds of mourning (e.g., Mic 1:8). The ostrich is a bird that seems unlike a bird; the hyena is not a dog but seems like a dog. The jackal, the true dog, is a skulking scavenger, known to swarm a kill as soon as its predators have finished eating and dispersed. All in all, the hyena, the jackal, and the ostrich are so strange that they are liable to turn the stomach.

Nevertheless, this trio has a place in GOD's Design. GOD incorporates them into His Word here at verse Revelation 18:2, and, in the end, He will call on some of them to fall permanently with Babylon. At verse Isaiah 43:20, to illustrate the reach of His grace, GOD shares that His grace will penetrate even through the jackal's and the ostrich's foul and hateful temperaments. At verse Lamentations 4:3, He points out that jackals nurse their young – though, fatefully, He does so without enthusiasm and only to show that the Israelites were failing to meet even minimal standards of kindness, having become "cruel, like the ostrich." Finally, as discussed chapter 2, He relies on an object lesson involving the ostrich to point Job in His direction (Job 39:13-18).

CHAPTER 6 "Faith in Ecclesiastes"

Colossians 2 - In the spirit of Ecclesiastes, Paul devotes the second chapter of Colossians to counseling the Colossians on the struggle between faith and reason. He exhorts them to allow the former to prevail in themselves.

CHAPTER 7 "Spirit"

Deuteronomy 29:29 - "The secret things belong to the LORD our GOD, but the revealed things belong to us and to our children forever, to observe all the words of this law." cf. Psalm 131:1

Hosea 2:18 - GOD promises to make a covenant with the animals not to harm the Israelites.

CHAPTER 8 "Christ's Words"

Genesis 3:1-15 - Together with Matthew 10:16, Genesis 3:1-15 is a compelling example of how an animal attribute can have dissimilar connotations in dissimilar contexts. The serpentine wisdom Jesus commends to the Apostles in Matthew is the very craftiness that ultimately led GOD, in Genesis, to condemn the serpent to eat dust all the days of its life.

Luke 15:3-10 - The Parables of the Lost Sheep and the Lost Coin. Jesus tailored the former to the men in his audience and the latter to the women.

Matthew 18:10-14 - The Parable of the Lost Sheep, inspired by children in Jesus's presence.

CHAPTER 9 "The Muzzled Ox"

Matthew 23:4 - Unlike Christ's (Mt 11:28-30), the Pharisees' yoke is straining.

1Timothy 5:18 - Another reference to Deuteronomy 25:4, as in First Corinthians 9:9-11.

CHAPTER 10 "Second Peter, Chapter 2"

Daniel 4:16, 5:21 - The prospect of being given the mind of an animal is ominous because of the inferiority of the animal mind to the human mind, cf. Psalm 32:8-9.

Isaiah 56:9-12 - One of the Bible's mentions of (potential) GOD-ordained animal predation on humans: an invitation to the wild animals to devour the torpid Israelites, with impunity.

1Kings 13:24 - as above. A lion justifiably kills a disobedient man of GOD.

1Kings 20:36 - as above. A lion justifiably kills a disobedient prophet.

2Kings 2:23-24 - as above. A group of small boys comes out of Bethel to jeer at Elisha, and forty-two of them are mauled by bears after Elisha curses them. (The Bible does not indicate why the adults of Bethel allowed the children to go outside the city on their own.)

Proverbs 26:17 - as above. Meddling in others' quarrels is likened to grabbing a passing dog's ears, leaving the meddlers themselves to blame for any injuries they suffer.

Psalm 63:10 - as above. GOD will reduce David's enemies to jackals' prey.

CHAPTER 13 "Suffering II"

Acts 8:32-35 - Philip imparts to the Ethiopian eunuch that Isaiah 53:7 is a prophecy of Jesus.

Isaiah 7:4 - Another reference to the practice of branding, as in Isaiah 50:11.

Jeremiah 12:3 - As Romans 8:36, below.

Mark 5:13 - Jesus possesses the swine, as in Luke 8:26-33.

Matthew 8:32 - as above.

Proverbs 11:22 - "Like a gold ring in a pig's snout / is a beautiful woman without good sense." Similar in tone to Jesus's "pearls before swine" analogy (Mt 7:6).

Romans 8:36 - A reference to the practice of separating sheep for slaughter, Romans 8:36 quotes Psalm 44:22. cf. Isaiah 53:7.

CHAPTER 14 "The Good Shepherd"

Ezekiel 34:11-16 - GOD portrays Himself as a shepherd.

Matthew 2:6 - Matthew quotes Micah's prophecy of the Shepherd Jesus (Mic 5:2-4).

CHAPTER 15 "Dominion II"

Romans 6:5-11 - Death no longer holds dominion over Christ or the faithful.

CHAPTER 16 "Hunting & Fishing"

2Kings 4:42-44 - Like Jesus, Elisha miraculously fed many with what seemed far too little.

Psalm 9:15-16 - More hunting-related images, as in Job 18:8-10

CHAPTER 17 "Diet"

Psalm 78:27-31 - An allusion to the quail-meat episode of Numbers 11.

CHAPTER 18 "Man v. Animal"

Leviticus 25:3-7 - GOD commands the Israelites to let their fields lie fallow once every seven years. GOD declares that whatever the land produces on its own will be food for the people, their livestock, and the wild animals. So, to the benefit of people and animals alike, the land will be recharged and all may eat.

CHAPTER 19 "Dominion III"

Psalm 112:4 & Psalm 116:5 - GOD and the faithful are gracious, merciful, and righteous.

Revelation 22:21 - The closing words of the Bible, "The grace of the LORD Jesus be with all the saints. Amen."

ALPHABETICAL INDEX OF VERSES

ABBREVIATIONS USED IN THIS BOOK

Acts - Acts
Am - Amos
1Chr - 1 Chronicles
2Chr - 2 Chronicles
Col - Colossians
1Cor - 1 Corinthians
2Cor - 2 Corinthians
Dan - Daniel
Deut - Deuteronomy
Ecc - Ecclesiastes
Eph - Ephesians
Ex - Exodus
Ezek - Ezekiel
Gal - Galatians
Gen - Genesis
Heb - Hebrews
Hos - Hosea
Isa - Isaiah
Jas - James
Jer - Jeremiah
Job - Job
Joel - Joel
Jn - John
1Jn - 1 John
2Jn - 2 John
3Jn - 3 John
Josh - Joshua
Jude - Jude
Judg - Judges
1Kings - 1 Kings
2Kings - 2 Kings
Lev - Leviticus
Lk - Luke
Mal - Malachi
Mk - Mark
Mt - Matthew
Mic - Micah
Neh - Nehemiah
Num - Numbers
Ob - Obadiah
1Pet - 1 Peter
2Pet - 2 Peter
Phil - Philippians
Prov - Proverbs
Ps - Psalms
Rev - Revelation
Rom - Romans
1Sam - 1 Samuel
2Sam - 2 Samuel
1Thes - 1 Thessalonians
2Thes - 2 Thessalonians
1Tim - 1 Timothy
2Tim - 2 Timothy
Zech - Zechariah

Printed in Great Britain
by Amazon

34415838R00050